# RURAL CHURCH TURNAROUND

# RURAL CHURCH TURNAROUND

### REAL LIFE EXPERIENCES OF RURAL PASTORS AND LAY-LEADERS

## Danny Davis

CrossLink Publishing

CrossLink Publishing
1601 Mt. Rushmore Rd, STE 3288
Rapid City, SD 57702

Ordering Information:
Quantity sales. Special discounts are available on quantity purchases by corporations, associations, and others. For details, contact the "Special Sales Department" at the address above.

Rural Church Turnaround/Davis —1st ed.

ISBN 978-1-63357-205-8

Library of Congress Control Number: 2019950838

First edition: 10 9 8 7 6 5 4 3 2 1

# Praise for Rural Church Turnaround

Everyone loves a good "comeback story". The rural church in North America is in desperate need of exactly that. With me, the light of the Gospel is beginning to fade from small towns across the nation. But the good news is there is hope! Jesus is still in the resurrection business...even when it comes to rural churches. In his book Rural Church Turnaround, Danny Davis shares stories of this hope as he outlines the principles and practices necessary for a rural church comeback story. I believe this book will inspire and encourage many leaders to see with fresh vision God's heart for their rural communities as they believe Him for their own comeback story.

Jon Sanders
Lead Pastor - The Rescue Church
Small Town Big Church Network

I've had the pleasure of knowing Danny for a few years now, and it didn't take long for me to realize he was going to be an incredible asset to rural church pastors. His new book Rural Church Turnaround just proves what I already knew. He is quickly becoming one of the leading voices in the rural church landscape. In this book Danny shares stories of pastors who inherited rural churches on the brink of collapse, and somehow brought them back. Each pastor's story of revival is unique, and yet you'll find yourself relating to each of their struggles and their moments of joy. This is a must-read for every rural church pastor.

Travis Stevens
Executive Pastor - Strong Tower Church
https://travisstephens.me

Dr. Davis's effort in compiling this resource is an answer to a personal prayer of mine. My life and ministry is a product of the rural church. Out of a sense of obligation and burden to "pay it back," I started investing in under-resourced rural pastors almost ten years ago. It was shocking how few resources were available specifically targeting the unique challenges of rural church leadership. I started praying that God would raise up capable men and women to fill that void. This book is an answer to prayer. Dr. Davis doesn't avoid the challenges and realities, but he leaves us hopeful about the future the rural church. With a touch of God's grace and adequate preparation of its leaders, the rural church can rise again.

Dr. Bryan Jarrett
Lead Pastor Northplace Church Sachse, Texas
Found/Director Lonesome Dove Ranch and
Water Tower Leadership Training
Billy Graham Center Rural Matters Institute Advisory Council

The imagery that came to mind as I read Danny Davis' book was a ship going through a tumultuous storm. In going through such a storm, the keys are to stable the ship, hold on to something secure, and have a courageous leader at the helm. Danny's book sure provides a blueprint for how struggling and declining rural churches can weather the storm of turnaround. While many churches attempt, very few arrive. And it is Danny's book that highlights the stories of those churches who attempted, arrived, and are now thriving.

Dr. Josh Laxton
Assistant Director of the Billy Graham Center
North America Lausanne Coordinator

*To my wife, Sherry, who has walked this journey of rural church turnaround with me. Her love and undying support never cease to amaze me. She and I have bounced around the world together pursuing the will of God and training leaders. Her ministry to children around the world has impacted eternity.*

*To all the pastors and lay leaders who pursue the calling of God in the forgotten places. You are my heroes! Every day you get up and go about your calling to equip people for ministry. You are on the frontlines of kingdom work—God's blessings to you.*

# Contents

# List of Tables & Figures

# Introduction

The death and decline of churches in America is a well-known problem in every denomination. Religious researchers estimate 65 to 80 percent of all churches in the United States have either plateaued or are declining.[1] Many of these churches are in rural areas. According to the National Congregations Study, church attendance in rural communities has dropped from 43.4 percent in 1998 to 31.7 percent in 2012, making it hard for churches to sustain the mission of God.[2] Yet every small town and rural community deserves a life-giving, vibrant church.

Pastors of rural churches face different difficulties in keeping their churches viable than their counterparts in urban and suburban areas, difficulties I have experienced firsthand. After serving as a church planter, pastor, and professor in Johannesburg, South Africa, for ten years, I accepted a call to pastor an established but dying Assemblies of God church in a rural western Missouri town with an approximate population of fifty-three hundred. Since 2013, several faithful lay leaders and I have clumsily led the church to initial stages of health and vitality. Although we have made significant progress, much remains to be done.

My experience in leading this rural church to turnaround aroused my curiosity and drove me to ask the question, "What are the experiences of other rural turnaround pastors and what can I learn from them?" And so, I began exploring the revitalization of rural churches. I focused on churches within my own denomination, the Assemblies of God, and within the state of

---

1 Clarensau, 2017; R. Houseal, personal communication, February 15, 2018; Rainer, 2017.

2 National Congregations Study, 2012. See Appendix, Tables 1–4.

Missouri. I also focused not only on the pastors and the qualities they possessed that helped them turn their churches around but also on the lay leaders within those churches whose efforts were just as essential in revitalization.

The problems facing my church were like those facing pastors in rural churches across America. Church turnaround is in large part a process of cultural change. Churches in decline tend to turn inward and go into survival mode. Moving congregations from an inward culture of self-preservation to one of vision for growth always necessitates radical change. Those changes create tension between pastors and lay leaders as they work through the implementation of and resistance to change, and so the relationship between these individuals is critical to the turnaround process.

I have not attempted to promote any one strategy or model of church revitalization. The uniqueness of each local congregation is too wonderful to force into a predetermined—and possibly irrelevant—ministry model. Instead, I relay the insights garnered from the experiences of pastors and lay leaders who are facing the challenges of plateauing and decline and are succeeding. Even though the churches featured in this book are all members of the Assemblies of God in southern Missouri, the principles and practices learned through their turnaround experiences can be applied in churches across most all evangelical traditions. I challenge you, the reader, to hear the stories of the pastors and lay leaders contained in these pages, compare them to your situation, and then do the hard work of applying what you've learned to your current situation. My hope is that these insights will provide denominational and church network leaders with a rich understanding of the challenges and the joys inherent in turning rural churches around and pastors and lay leaders with encouragement and help in doing so.

# CHAPTER 1

# The Decline of the Rural Church

Across the United States, small church buildings dot the rural landscape, churches that have served as the center of spiritual life within their communities for generations.[3] The people in these congregations meet faithfully each Sunday to worship God and fellowship with one another. Here, they marry, inform their children's spirituality, mourn their loved ones, and participate in multitudinous pot-luck dinners. However, many of these churches are in the throes of decline and may not exist long without the intervention of strong pastoral leadership.

The information on church growth presents a bleak picture for churches of all denominations. An estimated 70 percent to 80 percent of churches in North America are "stagnant or declining."[4] In the largest evangelical denomination in the United States, 65 percent of Southern Baptist churches are plateaued or declining.[5] Within the Church of the Nazarene, 51 percent of its churches declined in 2017.[6] The statistician for the General Council of the Assemblies of God reports 70 percent of its churches in the United States are plateaued or declining.[7]

---

3 Damon, 2018.
4 Stetzer and Dodson, 2007, 19.
5 Rainer, 2017.
6 R. Houseal, personal communication, February 15, 2018.
7 Clarensau, 2017.

In rural areas, the picture is even bleaker. According to Russell, "Many of the 7,000 churches that close each year in America are in rural settings [and] thousands more are either in decline or struggling to survive."[8] Church attendance here has continued to drop, decreasing from 43.4 percent in 1998 to 31.7 percent in 2012;[9] and 75 percent of the people living in rural America do not attend church.[10]

But what constitutes a plateauing or declining church? Churches, like other organizations, have a typical life cycle. They begin with a dream and typically die within five decades.[11] Quantitatively, plateauing and decline are measures of actual worship attendance, not church membership. Rainer contends "church membership is fast becoming a meaningless metric."[12] We are all familiar with—or possibly lead—a church claiming hundreds on "the role," but our parking lots are empty on Sunday mornings (except for Christmas and Easter, of course). A plateauing church is flat in its worship attendance, having neither grown nor declined over a five-year period. Clarensau defines plateauing Assemblies of God churches as those that have neither grown more than 10 percent nor declined more than 10 percent over a five-year period.[13] Definitions of a declining church are a bit more varied.

Stetzer and Dodson define a declining church as one having growth of 10 percent or less over a five-year period.[14] Martin defines a declining church as one experiencing a minimum of a 5 percent decline in average church attendance over a ten-year period.[15] Costner and Penfold both define a declining church as

---

8  Russell, 2014.

9  National Congregations Study, 2012. See Appendix, Tables 1–4.

10  Hoskins, 2017.

11  Ross, 2013.

12  Rainer, 2017, para 7.

13  Clarensau, 2017.

14  Stetzer and Dodson, 2007.

15  Martin, 15

one having an average annual growth rate of -2.5 percent over a five-year period.[16]

In terms of Assemblies of God churches, the Southern Missouri District Council of the Assembly of God reports a total of 360 local congregations in all the counties south of the Missouri River.[17] Of those churches, 163 are considered rural churches, located in cities with populations of five thousand or less. These small town and rural churches have experienced a 12 percent average overall decline in attendance from 2012 to 2017. These data reflect national and statewide trends of decline in many Assemblies of God churches.

Qualitatively, plateauing or declining churches are often described as having "lost momentum"[18] or as developing an attitude of "mere survival."[19] In a recent interview on the *Small Town Big Church Podcast*, I was asked to paint a picture of a church needing turnaround. I began with the numbers mentioned previously because it's easy to quote percentages, but the podcast host pressed me to describe a dying church without the numbers. In the moment, all I could think of were churches where the gospel has ceased to be the focus of their existence. Churches where political agendas and programs had replaced a heartfelt love for those who do not know Christ. Churches where budgets center upon maintaining and satisfying the current members and virtually no dollars are allocated for evangelism. In churches needing turnaround, members turn inward to maintain their memories of an idealized and often untrue past. They close ranks, enter survival mode, and become less welcoming of newcomers. This perfect storm of loss and nostalgia results in the stagnation, decline, and death of rural churches.

---

16 Costner, 2017; Penfold, 2011.
17 Nancy Cook, personal communication, August 3, 2018.
18 Mays, 2011, 9.
19 Ross, 2013, 4.

The very fact that churches are located in rural areas makes them more vulnerable to plateauing and decline. *Rural* is a multifaceted concept not based solely on population numbers but also on other more qualitative factors. Government agencies have twenty-four different definitions for the term "based on administrative, land-use, or economic concepts, exhibiting considerable variation in socio-economic characteristics and well-being of the measured population."[20] Depending on which of the definitions one uses, the percentage of United States residents living in rural areas ranges from 17 percent to 49 percent.

A rural location is also defined as "any population, housing, or territory not in an urban center."[21] Based on this definition, 97 percent of the United States population live in rural areas.[22] The Economic Research Center of the United States Department of Agriculture defines rural as "areas compris[ing] open country and settlements with fewer than 2,500 residents."[23] According to the National Association of Realtors, new criteria created and published in 2017 indicate locations are deemed "rural in character" if they have "a population between 2,500 and 10,000."[24] For instance, New Life Church–Farmington, whose story you will read later, is considered rural even though the town has a population of eighteen thousand people. Why is it considered rural? Simply put, it is situated a great distance from any urban or metro area. Rural is always defined by its proximity to more densely populated areas.

Population size is only the first piece of the definition puzzle, however. The second pertains to how rural areas compare to urban areas in population density and infrastructure. An urban area is large and densely populated, with people living close to

---

20 Cromartie and Bucholtz, 2008, para. 1
21 U.S. Census Bureau, n.d.
22 U.S. Census Bureau, 2016.
23 U.S. Department of Agriculture, 2013, para 7.
24 Harris et al., 2017, para. 2.

each other and with more and better infrastructure. Rural areas are less dense and sparsely populated and have less infrastructure, both in types and quality of these organizational structures. According to Ratcliffe et al., "After defining individual urban areas, rural is what is left."[25] In other words, *rural* is defined not by what it is but by what it is not. Demographer Kenneth Johnson offers this description of "what is left":[26] "manufacturing parks, warehouses, and food processing plants strung along rural interstates; sprawling exurban expanses just beyond the outer edge of the nation's largest metropolitan areas; regions where generations have labored to extract, process and ship coal, ore, oil, and gas to customers near and far; timber and pulp mills deep in rural forests; industrial towns struggling to retain jobs in the face of intense global competition; and fast-growing recreational areas proximate to mountains, lakes and coastlines."

Ethnically, rural United States is still predominantly White, although in-migration is increasing its racial diversity. From 1990 to 2004, the number of Hispanics living in rural areas nearly doubled. Slight increases in the numbers of African American and non-Hispanic Whites also occurred. Ethnic in-migration, however, does not offset the out-migration of people under the age of twenty.[27]

Since the 1970s, young adults have steadily migrated away from rural areas in search of better social, economic, and educational opportunities. The Rural Matters Institute offers several reasons for this out-migration of young adults:

- Poverty: In rural areas, 16.2 percent of adults and 23 percent of children live at or below the poverty line.
- Education: Rural schools often perform below average on national educational assessments.

---

25 Ratcliffe et al., 2016, 3.

26 Johnson, 2017, para. 3.

27 Kandle and Cromartie, 2004; Johnson, 2006.

- Mental health services: Two thirds of rural communities have a shortage of qualified mental health professionals.
- Political underrepresentation: Lawmakers allocate fewer and fewer federal dollars to rural communities: "People living in the rural heartland are left underserved and disregarded, despite having the same needs as those in other areas."[28]

This out-migration has also led to declining birth rates in most rural areas. As a result, "For the first time, rural counties as a whole are declining in population,"[29] with an estimated 40 percent having experienced depopulation since 2000.[30] The few rural counties experiencing growth are either located near urban centers or provide recreation, amenity, or retirement opportunities that attract newcomers.[31]

Much church decline has arisen from this rapid depopulation of rural areas, which creates numerous challenges for pastoral and lay leaders of rural congregations. As young adults exit, church membership and finances decline. The resulting aging congregations can no longer support ministry departments once vital to church life because the church can neither staff nor fund them. Fewer program offerings make the church less appealing to nonmembers.[32]

The migration of young adults from rural areas has also caused church planting organizations to place heavy emphasis on starting new churches in urban/suburban areas. Although these organizations are not wrong in their commitment to planting churches in these areas, my conversations with dozens of rural pastors show these pastors feel abandoned. Denominations

---

28 Rural Matters Institute, 2017, 3.
29 Cromartie, 2013, 6.
30 Johnson, 2006.
31 Johnson, 2006; Whitner and McGranahan, 2003.
32 See Farley et al., 2005; McIntosh, 1999.

and networks seem to have forgotten rural churches still exist as they define their success as organizations on "bodies, budgets, and buildings."[33]

Rural churches, in the main, are small yet constitute 52 percent of all churches and the majority of Evangelical churches in the United States.[34] Yet pastoral success is frequently—and I believe unfairly—measured in terms of worship attendance numbers. Even pastors involve themselves in the numbers game. Despite an average weekly church worship attendance in the United States of seventy-five people, whenever pastors get together, their favorite question of each other concerns how many people were in Sunday's worship service.[35] Leaders of declining churches often feel ashamed by their situations and resist taking nose counts each week.[36] These pastors may avoid speaking of decline by focusing on high attendance days, such as Easter and Christmas. They seem to think if they stop counting, their feelings of failure will also stop. I know personally the temptation to avoid counting "noses and nickels." In 2013, I became the pastor of a rural church whose weekly attendance had dropped from nearly two hundred to twenty in less than ten years.

---

33 Stetzer and Rainer, 2010, 28.
34 Dudley and Roozen, 2001.
35 National Congregations Study, 2012. See Appendix, Tables 1–4.
36 Vaters, 2018.

# CHAPTER 2

# Life Point Church

Odessa, Missouri is a small town of fifty-three hundred residents. Located thirty miles east of Kansas City, Missouri, off Interstate 70, Odessa's residents are mostly hard-working, blue-collar people who have chosen to raise their families away from the city. The school district has a wonderful reputation and serves as the center of activity in the town. Odessa football, baseball, softball, and basketball games offer residents opportunities to gather and cheer on their Bulldogs while catching up with friends. In 2013, I accepted the pastorate of Odessa First Assembly of God, where I continue to serve.

The first time I drove through Odessa's downtown, most businesses were closed and many historical buildings were boarded up. A church member told me of a pastoral candidate who, upon driving through the boarded-up downtown, decided not to show up for church. The candidate later called a deacon to explain that, upon seeing just how dead the town was, he felt it best to withdraw from the list of potential pastors.

Today, the town has seen an amazing revitalization of its downtown. Business owners are restoring buildings, opening their doors, and adding immense value to our little town. Today, if you drive through downtown, you will find a beautiful and busy eclectic mix of coffee shops, diners, antique stores, and an ice cream parlor.

Odessa First Assembly of God was officially organized in 1969, although it started as an independent Pentecostal work in 1938. However, the church never seemed to get established, opening and closing as pastors came and went. Once as I was reading through church records, I found a list of dozens of pastors' names with the dates of their service. Dates for some pastors were simply question marks because no one remembered these pastors' names or their pastoral work. For others, descriptions using physical characteristics of the pastor took the place of forgotten names. I estimated more than three dozen pastors had attempted to lead this church but had soon moved on. Some of them had lasted only a few weeks, some a few months, and others a few years.

When the church organized as an Assemblies of God congregation, it began to find stability. The church purchased the property they had been renting for Sunday worship. Then, in 1978, they purchased the land we still own today. In 1979, they built a church building, complete with offices and educational space. Under solid pastoral leadership, the church grew to about two hundred people and added a second building in 2000. Then something happened and the church began to falter: A popular and long-standing pastor resigned for health reasons, and the church struggled to find its footing after his departure.

The church elected a new pastor who stayed less than eighteen months. According to a former deacon, the pastor literally announced his resignation and walked out the side door of the auditorium, leaving the congregation in shock. Unable to govern itself, Odessa First Assembly was placed into the care of the Southern Missouri District leadership. They appointed an interim pastor and the church stabilized; but, after two years, the interim pastor resigned because of bad health. Again, the church was without pastoral leadership. Depending on various ministers to fill the pulpit each Sunday, the church declined further. A once thriving congregation had dwindled from approximately two hundred members to about twenty-five. When my family and I arrived on location, the church was at its lowest point financially, numerically, and spiritually.

I was expected to preach both the morning and evening Sunday services during my "try out" for the church. When my family and I arrived for the evening service, we were met at the door by a church attendee. This person had not been present in the morning service and did not know us. As we entered, the attendee said, "Glad you are visiting us tonight; but honestly, this is probably not where you want to go church." When I explained my reason for visiting, the embarrassed attendee apologized for the comment and quickly went away. I knew at that moment God was calling us to this little church, sensing God was showing me He would bring life to what seemed dead.

Some ten years before becoming the pastor of Odessa First Assembly, God had given me a dream of the building and the people. I had forgotten that dream until I was leaving my office one day. It had been a very tough day of dealing with some upset members. As I closed my office door and slid the key into the lock, the dream rushed back into my memory. I knew then God had placed me and my family here and He would supply our every need.

The church facilities were worn and outdated. Unattractive hand-me-down furniture filled the lobby. The building smelled like a strange mixture of mold and wet paper because stacks of outdated magazines were stored under a desk in the lobby meant to be a welcome center for guests. The carpets were rotting and dusty from lack of maintenance. The bathrooms, once bright and inviting, were dreadful and malodorous, replete with torn linoleum, ripped wallpaper, faded paint, and a stench left from malfunctioning toilets. Well-intentioned members had tried to find the cheapest way possible to maintain the facilities but just could not keep up. Strangely, however, many of the church members did not seem to notice these issues. If they were cognizant of the maintenance issues and general shabby appearance of the building, they never brought it up in conversation.

Most of the small congregation's members were elderly. Many had faithfully served the Lord for more years than I had lived. One long-standing member, commenting on the age of the members, said, "Pastor, our church is six funerals from dead!" They had seen pastors with vision come and go. They had lived with change initiatives implemented by pastors who did not stay around long enough to see the change through to completion. They suffered what might be called "vision fatigue." In other words, I was just another guy with a vision for change who, like other previous pastors, would leave in the face of resistance. I am convinced the congregation was not antichange; they just knew they were dying. These wonderful people of God knew instinctively that without drastic change, the future of the church was in peril.

I viewed myself as a leader whose primary job was to assist others in embracing and navigating cultural change. Therein lay the tension. The congregation had, because of their recent history, adopted the attitude of "most change initiatives fail."[37] I reflexively took an opposing position, saying, "Change is good and necessary, no matter your experience." The challenge then was building a bridge between knowing the necessity of change and coming to agreement about what change meant. One thing we agreed on was the need for a third-party facilitator to help us come to a consensus on the meaning of change. I chose to employ the help of the Church Transformation Initiative to facilitate a one-year process called The Acts 2 Journey. The Acts 2 Journey helps church leaders assess current realities through collaborative processes, assessment tools, and discussion groups.

Over our one-year period, the church leadership team and I walked through an intentional process of discovering each other's

---

37 Fullan, 2011, 5.

worldview about how the church should function. The team was asked to consider definitions for five key characteristics of a healthy church: service, growth, connecting, going, and worshiping. These characteristics are not random; they are derived from the Apostle Luke's description of the first-century church in Acts 2:42-46. In facilitating three brainstorming sessions with the church leadership to discuss these five characteristics, I wrote each attribute at the top of a poster-sized sheet of paper and hung each on the wall. The team members were asked to say the first thing that came to their minds when reading the words *worship*, *serve*, *go*, *grow*, and *connect*. We handled each characteristic individually until the team felt they had adequately described their thoughts on each of the five characteristics. There were no rules of order that might restrict creativity; and I wrote down every thought, word, idea, and remark on the appropriate paper. Some of the papers became large blocks of black ink scribbles, making sense only to the participants. This brainstorming exercise helped us to discover both points of agreement and points of disagreement about the mission of the church in the world.

At the end of our third meeting, the team asked me to craft concise definitions of the five characteristics based on their input. Once finished, I distributed the resulting document to team members and asked them to write down comments and suggestions regarding changes they wanted to discuss at the next meeting. When we met again, we spent hours rewriting my definitions according to the team's contributions until we reached consensus. Next, we took time to reflect on how our work aligned with Scripture. We were then ready to move forward to develop a shared vision for change.

Simply talking about these characteristics and defining them was not enough. We had to begin the process of transformation that would put us back on the road to congregational health. This was a task we were not fully equipped to do, and so the team agreed to ask for help from a third party, an experienced coach.[38] Coaches help individuals and teams gain perspective on what seems like an overwhelming job of bringing about whole-scale change initiatives. According to Ogne and Roehl, "Coaching . . . enables transformation, which in turn leads to missional ministry. Great coaches come alongside leaders so that leaders can be transformed into the image of Christ and join Him on His redemptive mission."[39] Even though communication on our team had not broken down, we required an outsider's help to assist us in identifying gaps and setting realistic and measurable goals.[40] This is what coaches do.

Robinson suggests an organization can reach its full potential when it is willing to "shake free" of ideas that are no longer relevant.[41] Our coach led us in a one-day discussion event, asking us questions to challenge us to let go of irrelevant ideas. These ideas weren't bad or unbiblical in themselves; but, in our context, they would not help us move forward to health. The coach also engaged us in robust dialogue to establish our change goals and priorities. Through these processes, we developed a strategy for moving forward based on a shared worldview of the church and its mission and our capacity to make the transformation from dysfunction to health. Now it was time to do what very few leaders and organization do: execute the plan.

"Strategies most often fail because they are not executed well."[42] All the work we had done as a team would be of no worth if we did not act on it. We soon discovered making plans was easier than the doing. As Sean Covey explains, "Whether you call it a strategy, a goal, or simply improvement effort, any initiative you as a leader drive in order to significantly move your team

---

38 Schmuck et al., 2011, 283.
39 Ogne and Roehl, 2008, 7.
40 Schmuck et al., 2011, 153.
41 Robinson, 2011, 7.
42 Bossidy and Charan, 2002, 15.

or organization forward will fall into one of two categories: The first is mainly a stroke of the pen; the second requires behavioral change."[43]

Our team had put pen to paper and formed a strategy. Now we had to ask the congregation to see the church, its mission, and the world around us differently. That meant changing minds about something vastly more important than the color of the auditorium carpet. We were asking congregants to see the community around them in a new way. We were challenging them to give up long-held preferences and consider what kind of church would attract new and younger members. Congregants had to reconsider what it meant to welcome "outsiders". These changes (and more) required current members to reconstruct practices that were second nature to them but foreign to the community we intended to engage.[44]

We began the path toward a revitalized church, and then it abruptly fell apart at the top. As change became real and tangible, leaders, many of whom were involved in formulating the change, decided it was too hard. They also decided I was too authoritarian, which may have been an accurate description of my leadership at this point. I was so focused on vision and turnaround that I had forgotten about the people. In my desperation to see the church grow, I pushed change at an unsustainable pace. The result was an exodus of many leaders and members as they saw opportunities to attach themselves to a minister with whom they felt more comfortable.

I was devastated. I begged God to release me from the pastorate of this "God forsaken church and town." Thankfully, God ignored my selfish pleas. Instead, He answered my prayers by sending us about a dozen new members from a church that had recently closed. That group of people, and many more who came later, picked up the vision of *connecting people to God, helping*

---

43 Covey, 2012, 3.
44 Cunningham, 2012, 54.

*people grow in their relationship with Christ, and going out in the power of the Holy Spirit*, and ran with it. God's provision of people showed me that He was involved in the resurrection of Life Point. God revealed to me that He loved Odessa and the church more than I did.

The years after the exodus have been fruitful. As of the writing of this book, the church is debt free. Through the generosity of our denomination and the help of various ministries, our facilities are remodeled. Leaders are stepping up and leading ministry teams. New ministry is being formed and carried out. A church once focused on survival is now actively involved in its community. We are not breaking attendance records but are seeing steady and sustainable spiritual and numerical growth.

To reflect this new vitality and identity, the congregation decided to change the name of the church to Life Point Church. The attendance at Life Point Church has grown to nearly sixty attendees each Sunday. More important, though, is our members' growth in their relationships with one another and with the community we are called to serve.

# CHAPTER 3

# Transformational Leadership and the Rural Church

Turning a plateauing or declining church around is rare and requires strong leadership to effect. Such pastoral leadership is both biblical and necessary for any church desiring to move from stagnation to health. In his letter to the Ephesians, Paul describes a five-fold ministry model instituted by Christ for equipping Christ-followers for "works of service."[45] The Ephesians leadership model identifies apostles, prophets, evangelists, pastors, and teachers.

Pastoral ministry includes caring for and teaching Christ-followers in a local context. The New Testament uses five words to describe the functional roles of a pastor: elder, bishop, shepherd, preacher, and teacher.[46] These descriptions highlight three biblical qualities of pastoral leaders. First, pastors are intentionally involved in the betterment of those under their care through preaching and teaching. Second, pastors guide the spiritual direction of a local church like a shepherd leads sheep. Third, as elder and bishop, pastors are overseers of the local church's administrative needs. These three qualities serve one goal: the equipping

---

45  Eph 4:11–12 (New International Version).
46  Maybue, 2005.

of Christ-followers for "works of service," which leads to the expected result of "the body of Christ [being] built up."[47]

Paul also teaches that, at conversion, all Christ-followers are given gifts by the Holy Spirit.[48] Pastors are, for lack of a better description, the boots on the ground assisting church members in discovering and utilizing the gifts given to them by the Holy Spirit. Then, through various educational means, pastors are to help believers develop their gifts for the benefit of the local assembly and the global Body of Christ.

Although the way pastors accomplish these tasks may have changed through the centuries, pastors who lead their churches to revitalization are fully aware of their biblical responsibilities. They also tend to embrace a transformational leadership style, which has been shown to be best suited to moving a church from plateau or decline to life and health, being "positively related to high church attendance among congregants and growth in church membership."[49] In addition, these pastors understand leading a rural church is different from leading a nonrural church and recognize the invaluable role of lay leaders in successfully turning around a dying church.

In his Pulitzer Prize winning book *Leadership*, MacGregor Burns outlines three types of leaders and their characteristics: laissez-faire, transactional, and transforming. Of the three types of leaders, transforming or, what is now called, transformational leaders are at the top of the scale. Laissez-faire leaders take a hands-off approach, leaving followers without clear direction and are, therefore, the least competent in the three styles. Transactional leaders are at the mid-point of the scale and lead by offering rewards to their followers who meet prescribed expectations. Although more effective than laissez-faire leaders, transactional leaders are still more concerned with their own interests

---

47  Eph 4:12 (NIV).
48  See 1 Cor 12:4—5; 1 Peter 4:10; Rom 12:4—6a (NIV).
49  Bass, 1990, 22.

and goals than those of their followers. Transformational leaders are the most effective leaders. They focus primarily on achieving mutually shared goals rather than self-interests. They cast vision with clarity and influence followers to share in that vision by promoting follower creativity and innovation,[50] "inspir[ing] followers to go beyond expected levels of commitment and contribution."[51]

Implicit in followers going beyond the expected is the element of personal and organizational change. Transformational leadership in any form is meant to change the "basic values, beliefs, and attitudes of followers."[52] Transformational leaders accomplish this through clearly articulating a vision of an optimistic and preferred future, showing followers how they can contribute to that vision, modeling the vision through behaviors that allow their followers to identify with them, stimulating followers to become creative and innovative, giving personal time to coach and mentor followers to assist them in their growth and development, and emphasizing the value of their followers above their self-interests.[53] Table 1 summarizes the qualities of transformational leaders pertaining to church revitalization.

### Transformational Qualities of Turnaround Pastors

| Quality | Source |
|---------|--------|
| Communicates God-given vision | Bass, 1985; Crandall, 1995; Hughes, 2014; Lamb, 2016; Martin, 2015; Penn, 2011; Penfold, 2011; Scuderi, 2010 |

---

50  Burns, 1978.

51  Rowold, 2008, 404.

52  Podsakof et al., 1990, 108.

53  Bass, 1999; Jandagh et al., 2008; Judge and Piccolo, 2004.

| | |
|---|---|
| Leads by example | Crandall, 1995; Nixon, 2004; Rainer, 2001 |
| Willingness to pay the price for change | Lamb, 2016; McEachin, 2011; Penfold, 2011; Stroh, 2014 |
| Commitment to stay at church | Ross, 2013; Martin, 2015 |
| Enables members to see the need for change | Lamb, 2016; Michaelis, Stegmaier, & Sonntag, 2010; Stroh, 2014 |
| The optimistic and faith-filled belief that the dying church can live | Frazee, 1995; Kouzes & Posner, 2017; Mays, 2011; Rainer, 2001 |
| Loves people helping them discover and develop gifts | Crandall, 1995; Nixon, 2004; Penfold, 2011; Rainer & Lawless, 2003 |
| Preaching/communication skills | Crandall, 1995; Penfold, 2011 |
| Personal faith and love for God | Crandall, 1995; Rainer, 2001 |
| Willingness to confront others in love | Lamb, 2016; Penfold, 2011; Wood, 2001 |

Table 1

All these characteristics of transformational leadership point to leaders who possess an ability to hold two truths in tandem: On one hand, these leaders are guided by compelling personal and organizational vision; on the other hand, they understand their vision cannot and must not be accomplished alone. Consequently, they not only inspire people to help them fulfill the vision but also empower and equip their followers to become autonomous leaders. The result is leadership multiplication as the primary leader gives away power and authority so that others are brought up and not kept down.

Turning around plateauing or declining churches requires immense and sometimes painful change. As Stroh states, "Turnaround is fairly rare . . . probably because it is often costly."[54] Churches who need revitalizing are often focused inwardly, thinking that by doing so they will survive. These congregations must be challenged to turn their eyes and hearts out to the communities they are called to serve. Doing so requires change, and turnaround pastors are committed to helping their members see the necessity of such change. They are further willing to "pay the price to lead change"[55] by helping their congregations see the realities of their current situation and moving them toward "patience, positivity, and passion."[56]

Thus, turnaround pastors must either be transformational leaders or learn to become transformational in their leadership approach. They must lead by effectively communicating a God-given vision to their followers and inviting them to share in that vision. Vision is key to motivating followers toward greater creativity, collaboration, and higher levels of performance. Turnaround pastors consistently cast a vision that compels people to act and challenges followers to deeper levels of organizational commitment. These pastors genuinely believe dying churches can live and, therefore, act tenaciously on those beliefs by painting the picture of a better future for their churches that are, for the moment, struggling to stay open for one more Sunday.

Turnaround pastors also have a number of other characteristics in common. They are focused, determined, outgoing, and energetic. They are innovative team leaders with excellent communication skills. They are able to leverage these attributes to direct transformational change in entrenched religious cultures. These pastors also have three characteristics essential to the turnaround process: the ability to manage emotional pain,

---

54 Stroh, 2014, 138.
55 Penfold, 2011, 175.
56 Lamb, 2016, 157.

a willingness to endure the inevitable personal crises that arise from cultural change, and a deep commitment to staying with their church anywhere from five to twelve years to effect the change needed to bring about revitalization.[57]

Perhaps the most important attribute of a turnaround pastor is a genuine love for people. When Jesus was asked, "Teacher, which is the greatest commandment in the Law," he answered, "'Love the Lord your God with all your heart and with all your soul and with all your mind.' This is the first and greatest commandment. And the second is like it: 'Love your neighbor as yourself.'"[58] For turnaround pastors, then, love is not an abstract or vague concept. Through the enablement of the Holy Spirit, they commit to typifying a life committed to these two commands and, in doing so, inspire their followers to do the same. In practical terms, then, turnaround pastors are authentic and lead by example. They maintain an elevated level of faith and optimism. They model a life of deep spiritual discipline. They take concrete action to build up their followers as Paul describes in Ephesians 4:11–12 by helping their congregants discover and develop their gifts and empowering them to use those gifts in shared ministry. They are also willing to confront others in love.

As transformational leaders, turnaround pastors understand their leadership priorities must take into account the culture and setting of the church. Although rural and nonrural pastors identify the same five pastoral tasks as essential (i.e., "visionary leadership, dynamic preaching, multi-generational discipleship, biblical knowledge, and culturally relevant outreach"[59]), they prioritize those tasks differently, as shown in Table 2.

---

57 See Penfold, 2011; Ross, 2013.
58 Matt 22:36–39.
59 Carney, 2010, 100.

## Ranking of Essential Pastoral Tasks of Rural and Nonrural Pastors

| Pastoral task | Rural ranking | Nonrural ranking |
|---|---|---|
| Dynamic preaching | 1 | 3 |
| Visionary leadership | 2 | 1 |
| Biblical knowledge | 3 | 4 |
| Multi-generational discipleship | 4 | 2 |
| Culturally relevant outreach | 5 | 5 |

Table 2

They also understand these churches do not function in the same ways urban/suburban churches do because of their size and settings, as this experience of a young pastor in Iowa assigned to a twelve-member congregation clearly shows: "I could put up office hours all day long in rural America, and nobody's coming. But if I sit on the combine with them, or go to the coffee shop, or watch a volleyball game with them—they don't want me to use the word 'counseling', but we talk through things."[60] When this young pastor adapted his leadership style to fit the context of this rural church, his membership increased from twelve to thirty. And so, pastors desiring to lead rural churches must adapt their leadership style to their context.

To do this, these pastors must understand the nature of power and control structures in rural churches. In other words, how things get done in small rural churches is different from larger nonrural churches. Small churches rely heavily on volunteers instead of paid staff to lead key initiatives and programs, so these churches must be relational rather than "rationally structured, task driven, goal-oriented organization[s]."[61] Even the most

---

60 Metaxes and Guthrie, 2017, para. 8.
61 Sprayberry, 2010, abstract.

capable pastor cannot produce church growth alone but must have the help of a capable and willing laity.[62]

The role of lay leaders is often mentioned but not well-defined by researchers, yet these volunteer members of the pastoral leadership team play a significant role in helping lead plateauing or declining rural churches to turnaround. If pastors mean to mobilize the church for God's mission effectively, they must elevate the role of lay leaders in the church. Doing so includes casting a clear vision that lay leaders can easily understand and that clearly calls laity to ministry involvement.

One of the most significant challenges facing churches may be the lack of trained lay leaders.[63] Turnaround pastors understand the biblical mandate given in Ephesians 4:11–12 to develop strong lay leadership, which makes revitalization possible. These pastors lift up the role of lay leaders within the church, involving them in significant ministry tasks and decision-making, equipping and inspiring their lay leaders to co-labor with them in a "synergistic" relationship.[64]

In examining turnaround rural churches, I assumed their pastors elicited from their lay leaders reverence, trust, and satisfaction with their leader. What I found was that these effects formed a unique group identity, resulting in higher performance than I initially expected. Turnaround pastors act in ways to influence their followers to higher levels of commitment and performance. They empower them to find innovative solutions and reach shared goals creatively. The results of such development and empowerment are "high capacity" lay leaders who possess four distinct qualities:[65]

---

62 See McEachin, 2011; Penfold, 2011.
63 Hunt, 2016.
64 Martin, 2015, abstract.
65 Costner, 2017, 133–34.

- They understand "their purpose and God's call on their life."
- They have "a growth mindset."
- They have "a servant's heart."
- They have "a desire to multiply and grow the body of Christ."

As such, they work alongside their pastors to achieve a shared, God-inspired vision for their church.

Despite the negative effects of the demographic shift from rural areas to urban centers and clusters, many rural churches are candidates for turnaround. After returning from Johannesburg, South Africa, I accepted the call at an established but dying rural church in western Missouri, Odessa First Assembly of God. My experiences in working with a faithful group of lay leaders to revitalize this church motivated me to examine other turnaround churches, focusing on the relationship between the pastor and lay leaders in the efforts of these churches to reverse the trend of death and decline.

Missouri is the seventeenth largest state in the United States, with a population of over six million. Over 50 percent of Missourians live in urban centers; 36.6 percent live in rural locations. Of its 114 counties, 101 are classified as rural, 51 of which experienced population decline between 2005 and 2015. The remaining 50 counties had either no change or a slight increase in population during the same period.[66]

The state is further divided into northern and southern Missouri, with the Missouri River serving as the line of demarcation. For more than a century, counties in the north have declined in population. According to Herrold, "Several north Missouri counties had three or four times as many people in 1900 as they did in 2010. Almost all north Missouri counties

---

66 Van Dyne et al., 2017.

have experienced significant population loss through the 20th Century and into the 21st."[67] Reasons for declining rural populations in this state are similar to those in the rest of the United States, including advances in agriculture, an older nonchildbearing population, out-migration of a younger population looking for better employment, and a lack of doctors and hospitals.[68]

The three other rural Missouri churches highlighted here have experienced the same kinds of plateauing and decline as thousands of others across the United States. They have, however, managed to turn their situations around, experiencing sustained increases in Sunday worship attendance. Understanding the situations these churches were in prior to their turnaround is essential to understanding just how far they have come and the impact of how they have managed to achieve these results.[69]

---

67 Herrold, 2017, para. 6.

68 Herrold, 2017; Mercer, 2012.

69 See Davis, 2019, for the structure of the hermeneutic phenomenological study that is the basis for this book.

# CHAPTER 4

# New Life Church–Barnett

For more than eight decades, New Life–Barnett has been serving its small community of 207 residents. The town is 168 miles from an urban center and nearly an hour's drive to the closest large city (population of approximately forty thousand). The massive brick and metal church building lies on a heavily trafficked rural state route. One cannot help but notice this monstrous building, with its well-maintained gravel parking lot, situated in open country with little else around it. Most of the church's land lies behind the building, including a small pond. Aerial photographs of the property that chronologically detail multiple phases of construction adorn a conference room wall.

A tour of the facilities conducted by one of the lay leaders reveals the members have been hard at work to create a comfortable space. According to Toni Montgomery, "Pastor always has a project for people to work on because we have a lot to keep up." A cleaning lady emerging from one bathroom greeted me with a smile and a handshake before going to the next bathroom. Upon complimenting her on how clean everything looked, she replied, "I love my job! I love what I get to do for God!" This woman had come to the church through its ministry for those struggling with addiction.

The enormous foyer sparkles as the glass front doors let in a generous amount of light. Large pews fill the high-ceilinged sanctuary, providing seating for more than two hundred wor-shippers. A well-decorated stage, backlit with LED lights (new features for this country church) takes up approximately 25 per-cent of the sanctuary floor. Musical instruments, a pulpit, and other typical church furnishings adorn the stage. A large media booth at the rear of the room houses audio and visual equipment operated on Sundays and Wednesdays by a team of volunteers. The building also houses a new café, well-equipped nurseries, multiple classrooms, and a gymnasium where more than one hundred children receive weekly meals and participate in age-appropriate church services. The church offices are relatively small compared to the areas set aside for people to gather.

This allocation of floor space reflects the church's vision for "connecting people to Jesus, teach[ing] them his ways, and sending them out to impact their neighbors, friends, and fam-ily." Pastor JD Montgomery recalled the initial reaction some church members had to removing walls to make room for a café where church attendees could meet, talk, and enjoy fellowship: "Everybody thought we were crazy. They were, like, you don't have a café in church!" Now it takes more than an hour for the building to empty after a Sunday service. This wonderful facility, however, has not always been a blessing.

To understand the turnaround process in New Life–Barnett, I interviewed not only the pastor but six lay leaders as a group. Four of the lay leaders had been members of the church for more than forty years. Three of them had come to the church in the 1970s and 1980s; the fourth had been a part of the church since childhood.

New Life–Barnett began as a home church. As it grew, the congregation moved to multiple locations in the area until it set-tled in its current site. The members had the vision to operate a school on the property as a ministry to the surrounding area. According to the pastor, "There were a good number of people [who] were faithful and diligent about [this] work over the years." Several of the lay leaders spoke to me fondly of seasons of growth and outreach the church had experienced through the years. David Cotton recounted a time in the 1980s when the church grew from 135 or 140 members to more than 240 people attending on Sundays. A jail ministry resulted in "thirteen guys being baptized in the creek in handcuffs." To care for the rapidly growing congregation, a group of five leaders held home services. David Cotton indicated the reason the church had moved was the need to have "two services a day" at the previous location. New Life–Barnett had also begun a Christian school and needed classroom space for its growing student population.

The successes soon became the focus of contention as jealousy overtook some members who felt neglected. Financial issues and the lack of teacher accreditation caused the school to falter and close. In 1993, a major church problem led to the resignation of the pastor. The new pastor elected stayed four years, the next pastor elected stayed only one and a half years, and long periods existed between these pastoral transitions that left the church without a senior leader. David Vernon, one of the lay leaders who operates a recovery ministry at New Life–Barnett, described the situation: "About the time things started to look up, the pastor would change, and everything would go through a change again and then start growing and then another change."

I asked this group of lay leaders why they chose to stay during all this turmoil. The question garnered several powerful responses from the group: "Because God was here," exclaimed Janice Sidebottom, a member of the church for multiple decades. Janice's husband, Raymond, responded, "God would not let me leave!" His statement was not one of desperation or angst about staying. He genuinely believed God had called him to serve New Life Church–Barnett, and he was obedient to that call. Helen Jarrett, who had grown up in the church and now served as the secretary, passionately stated, "We were family!" David Cotton, a soft-spoken lay leader, simply said, "We just had to tough it out."

Helen explained how God had given a vision to a trusted member's dad "about this property, and this church being here. You know, this is our home church, and we couldn't leave." Janice described how these tumultuous times drove the congregation to seasons of prayer: "Everyone started praying for our finances and for a pastor that could lead us, and God came through!" The answer to Janice's and the others' prayers was Pastor JD and his wife, Toni.

These long-standing members spoke honestly about the frequent pastoral leadership problems. Though most chose their words carefully, they described former pastors as being "womanizers," "having multiple affairs," having "serious women problems," and being "bad with dollars." Pastor JD described one such issue:

> In 2008, [the pastor] just got in the same trap that many people get in. I'll borrow ten dollars this week and pay it back next week, and next week you needed thirty dollars, and the next week it is more. Then finally he got into a place where he couldn't pay it back. The church bills hadn't [been] paid for a year. And there was no accounting for that money. The finances were fraudulent. So, all the board reports and the statements had been modified. So, it looked like everything was taken care of, but only this pastor and his wife were aware of what was going on.

With great humility, David, who was serving as a deacon at the time, recounted this same story in greater detail:

> In 2008, . . . [after] we had mortgaged the church to the bank in town—the loan officer called [me] and said, "You have a problem."

*"What's the problem?"*

*"The payments aren't being made. You're five months behind on your payments."*

*"Okay." We had a District man, and I called him and said, "I need to come and visit with you." I went to his office and, just as I sat down, his phone rang. The pastor at that time called and said, "What's my deacon doing in your office?"*

*"I don't know, he just come in, what's the problem?"*

*"Well," the pastor said, "he doesn't belong there."*

*I told the District man, "The loan officer called me from the bank, said you're five months behind and we're going to put a chain on the gate."*

*The District man said to the pastor, "I want you to call the bank, and you talk to that loan officer, and you find out what's going on!" [The District man] come back and said, "I don't believe it."*

*I said, "I believe it. I understand and know what's going on. The money is being stolen."*

The lay leaders who were attending the church during this time described themselves as "heartbroken" because they were in a building project and the church was experiencing some growth. Pastor JD and several lay leaders spoke of this event as causing the church to lose integrity with the membership, the community, and local businesses. Janice, however, positively and boldly declared, "But we knew God didn't lead us this far to leave us!"

Eventually, this pastor resigned, and the Southern Missouri District leadership appointed an interim pastor as an intervening measure. His task was to stabilize the church, which he accomplished. David Vernon described that period as "more focused on just keeping [the church] stable. Getting repairs done and doing the things that haven't been able to be done because of the finances." By 2014, dwindling church attendance had plateaued at approximately thirty people. The stabilizing influence of the interim pastor had helped the church to survive.

That same year, the interim pastor asked one of his friends to consider becoming the next pastor of New Life–Barnett. Despite having no experience as a senior pastor, Pastor JD agreed to do so, stating he felt God calling him to take this leap of faith.

Pastor JD had not come to vocational ministry through the usual path. He had no formal seminary training but had grown up attending Assemblies of God churches in and around a large urban center. His grandfather had even served as his pastor during his childhood. Pastor JD had also attended a larger inner-city church and later had served as a youth pastor in a rural Assemblies of God church.

Pastor JD excelled at business and had spent most of his working life honing his leadership skills in the corporate world. He was then serving as an executive for an organization with sixteen thousand employees. After accepting the leadership position at New Life–Barnett, he continued to work in the corporate world. He accepted no salary for his work with the church and commuted, along with his wife, Toni, nearly four hundred miles round trip each weekend for three years. Pastor JD felt his corporate leadership experience has been an asset in leading New Life–Barnett:

> You know, in the corporate world people would say to me, "You have a cult over there because these people would follow you into a burning building." Well, they were following me because they knew they'd be safe, and they knew I wouldn't let the corporate world come down on them. I think that's the same truth in the church. They know they are safe. They know I've got their back. And, as a leader, I think that's my

*role. It's not to do everything. It's not to be the boss.*
*It is to lead them and to ensure that they know they*
*are safe and that they have a place of security.*

When asked about the challenges of living in such a remote area, Pastor JD remarked, "Part of my responsibility is being there with [church members]. If somebody is sick, if somebody is dying, or somebody needs prayer—part of my responsibility is to be there to be able to touch and feel and be a part of that. And so, having the amount of space that people are away from each other limits my ability and my time to do that."

Soon after accepting the pastorate, Pastor JD received a call from the propane company refusing to extend any more credit to the church because the previous year's bill still had not been paid. The pastor soon learned the church owed nearly $10,000 in back payments to several vendors, including the propane company, a fact he did not know prior to accepting the position. However, the crisis became an opportunity for Pastor JD to demonstrate to the congregation his willingness to act on their behalf and to settle problems he had no hand in creating. In the process, he established trust and respect with the small congregation. Pastor JD described what happened next: "You know, we just, we just really began to pray. I was very honest with the people about where we were. They were very dedicated people. They were giving people, but they were tapped out of resources. And so. we just really had to pray that God would do something miraculous and He did. And so, we worked out a deal with the gas company that we would make the payments, and we would have it paid off within a month. And we were able to do that!" He then leaned forward in his chair and, with a smile on his face, continued to share the story of God's miraculous intervention: "We had a young couple that came and gave us a big boost. They had been in a very tragic car accident and had got a settlement, and they tithed on it. And so, that allowed us to get in a go forward position, and we kept doing that!"

Pastor JD further demonstrated his belief that this dying church could live by petitioning the Southern Missouri District to intervene. Assemblies of God ministers affiliated with the Southern Missouri District are required to pay 50 percent of their tithe to the District organization. Pastor JD asked the District to allow him to give 100 percent of his tithe to the church and they agreed. Because he still served as an executive of a large corporation, his tithe coming into the small church helped bridge a large financial gap.

Describing his personality and communication style as being "terribly blunt and very out front," Pastor JD kept the financial situation in front of the people. He knew the church had to establish a spending plan to move in a positive direction and believed that if a leader sets high expectations, followers will live up to those expectations. He appealed to their higher sense of purpose by telling them that by not paying their bills, they were putting God's integrity on the line. And he challenged them to think creatively about how the church could save money.

The massiveness of the church building was draining the church treasury. The costs of propane to heat, electricity to cool, and basic maintenance were more than the congregation of thirty could sustain. Pastor JD's transparency helped members see the need for change, making it easier to take some drastic cost reduction measures: "We closed off half the building that first winter I was here. I had a good friend of mine come in, and we determined that we could drain all the pipes in the back and shut that down. Then we could concentrate on heating the front of the building for the winter. That saved us about $4,000. I locked the back doors and shut the front [of the building] off, and that is how we survived the first winter." The lay leaders interviewed agreed not only that the congregation saw this measure as good but also that the action revealed the severity of their financial situation and caused people to "come through" financially.

Having taken care of the most immediate needs, Pastor JD turned his focus to establishing a good financial foundation for the future. The church, for the first time, established a budget and built a six-month cash reserve to sustain them in case of emergency. Again, Pastor JD appealed to a higher cause. By taking the financial actions he was recommending, should they experience tough times again they could keep their good name in the community and be a solid witness for Christ.

Pastor JD's transparency concerning financial matters and the positive fiscal actions to reduce spending and create a firm financial foundation catalyzed a new synergy in the congregation. A new identity began to form as the congregation began to take ownership and think differently about how people outside perceived the church: "Church people came up to me and said, 'Pastor JD, if we can't pay the electric bill, I will pay it!'"

Helen Jarrett eloquently described the congregation's perceptions of Pastor JD's leadership during this financial crisis: "We were just glad he was honest with us about the financial part of it, and everybody was on board because he knows money. I mean he knows how to manage it. We just wanted what was best for the church and how to move forward with that. He knew how to do that. So, everybody was just in agreement. You know he was . . . he was bold. He told us the truth. We wanted the truth and that . . . and that's just what anybody wants."

While working with the financial crisis, Pastor JD simultaneously began dealing with internal problems by establishing new expectations for public worship. Assemblies of God churches are Evangelical and Pentecostal. They believe in supernatural manifestations of the Holy Spirit, such as tongues and interpretation, words of wisdom and knowledge, and public prophetic utterances. Assemblies of God churches believe these supernatural gifts work to build up God's people and are to be exercised in an orderly manner. At New Life–Barnett, however, chaos rather than order was the rule, as Pastor JD described: "You know one of the [issues] was chaos. So not having a leader, everyone was a leader, and so it became clear that we needed to address that. And so, you know, you may have somebody jumping up in service and saying, 'Oh, I've got a word!' You had people just shouting out in the most bizarre ways [during worship service]."

Pastor JD knew this chaos in public worship had to be corrected and brought into alignment with biblical protocal and church vision. The current practice was a hindrance both to the saints benefitting from these supernatural gifts and to church growth. Pastor JD confronted this problem with love and a firm conviction the church had to change culturally if new people were to come and stay. He also knew some of the congregants would think he was "quenching the Spirit." This is a pejorative phrase used in Pentecostal circles in reference to someone who restricts the exercise of superatural gifts in a public worship service. In my nearly thirty years of ministry in Pentecostal churches, the accusation of "quenching the Spirit" comes from those who disagree with a new model or order of the public worship service that removes them from the limelight.

Pastor JD just kept the vision of connecting people to Jesus in the forefront and dealt with the problem of chaos through teaching: "Part of my responsibility was teaching, albeit difficult, that God deserves order and He's a gentleman. He doesn't interrupt. He doesn't send twelve messages for the same day. He brings clarity. He doesn't bring confusion." He also lovingly confronted members whose actions brought confusion to the congregation: "We had to call some of it out, and I think that was a culture shock because people thought it was okay not to be prepared for service." And so, Pastor JD set a new expectation of order that allowed for the public exercise of spiritual gifts but kept in mind people in attendance at Sunday worship who were unfamiliar with such practices.

A second internal issue in public worship concerned music: "I had people on the worship team here that couldn't sing. That wasn't their calling. It wasn't their gifting, but they loved being on the platform. Then as you try to improve and become the best music you can for the ears of our God—that was a rubbing point." Pastor JD approached this challenge in much the same way he did others: head on, with love and an appeal to a higher cause: "When I began to say let's determine what your gifting is, and I don't think it's this because we're not going to be able to accomplish our vision if we continue this, that created some noise. And that created people [who] were complaining and saying, 'But that's my uncle, and he's been on that team for 40 years!' But your uncle is deaf now, and he can't sing. So, let's get serious. You must be very resolute."

Pastor JD believed his resoluteness to stay on task and keep the vision in front of the people helped create an atmosphere of "self-selection." As he stayed true to the vision for the music ministry and kept appealing to a standard of excellence, people began to realize they had talents that were a better fit in other areas of service. So they removed themselves from one ministry and joined another, minimizing confrontation and conflict. This cultural change led to a music ministry that holds auditions two times per year and now requires team members to sign a yearly contract clearly outlining the expectations for their participation.

When I asked the group of lay leaders to pinpoint a moment when they knew things were going to improve, they looked at each other, waiting to see who would speak first. Finally, as David Vernon began to explain it was not a single moment but multiple moments along the way, the other leaders nodded in agreement. He also spoke of Pastor JD's consistency in preaching vision, and all agreed that his ability to cast vision was vital to their revitalization. Helen Jarrett spoke of Pastor JD's vision-casting ability in dramatic fashion: "[He] lights something up inside us," sparking excitement in people to get involved in various church ministries.

Janice Sidebottom spoke of God's intervention in their situation as a result of prayer: "We started with a lack of prayer apparently for things to just fall apart, and then when we started praying, as a body together, then it came alive." Crisis moments in the church catalyzed prayer. David Cotten recalled a situation in the early 1990s during a building project when money and promised donations of labor did not materialize. Turmoil over the situation negatively impacted the church, which "went from 130 members to 18 or 19 . . . [but] it was prayer that helped hold us together." He went on to explain that prayer was a tool that brought about increased volunteerism in the church. The need for volunteers resulted in seasons of prayer; and, miraculously, someone would volunteer: "We needed someone to drive a van, so we prayed and God answered. Then we needed a bus driver and God answered again!"

All the lay leaders agreed the key to the church's turnaround was a change of attitude toward ministry. Ministry became something one would "plant and give away." Instead of having a few individuals leading everything, the goal became leader multiplication. The need to multiply ministry meant some lay leaders surrendered leadership positions they had held for many years. In other cases, it meant beginning ministries with the intention of equipping and empowering someone else to lead it eventually. Pastor JD recounted the story of Janice Sidebottom, who led virtually every ministry in the church. Although vital to the future success of the church, Janice was also worn out. Pastor JD approached her, explaining that by doing everything, she was "stealing opportunities from everyone else." The pastor then worked with Janice and the other lay leaders to build a culture of replication, appealing to a higher cause by asking church leaders to always have a replacement so ministry would continue in their absence.

I asked the group of lay leaders to describe the most no-ticeable change at New Life–Barnett since Pastor JD's arrival. Without a moment's hesitation, David Vernon stated, "The big change I am seeing since Pastor JD's been here is that we are outside of the church more than inside of the church." New Life–Barnett has grown from thirty attendees to an average of three hundred in attendance at Sunday worship in the last five years. One of the first areas of major growth came from the Wednesday night youth ministry. As new people came into the church and received Christ as Savior, they were taught and then expected to go out and reach other people for Christ. That vision and ex-pectation resulted in people stepping up to drive the church van to bring youth to services. After that van and another filled up, the church purchased a school bus. As of this writing, 100 to 120 youth attend the Wednesday evening youth activities and church service. Volunteers provide meals for all youth in attendance, and youth also receive nonperishable items to take home to en-sure they have something to eat between services. The children's ministry has also taken off for New Life–Barnett, with about fifty children currently attending Sunday School and being involved in the children's church ministry.

New Life–Barnett serves an impoverished community, with many residents depending on social services, such as welfare and disability, to survive. Pastor JD described the situation vividly: "There's a lot of drugs and a lot of alcoholism. People are living on disability or off the government; then, of course, they are not getting the nutrition and health or the things they need because they're typically hocking those things to buy cigarettes, alcohol, and drugs. So, bad dental care, bad hygiene, and all those things. We have kids that come on Wednesdays that their parents are living in their cars and the only clean things these kids are getting is when they come here." Pastor JD's desire is to change the cul-tural expectations of not just the church but also the community through these ministries, noting that the "career aspirations" of most young people in the community are "growing up and getting on disability."

David Vernon pioneered a highly-successful biblically-based recovery ministry at New Life–Barnett. The ministry "is a multifunction ministry reaching those with addictions and those affected by addiction." Each week, thirty to forty adults gather to participate in an interactive Bible study and to hear stories of how others have overcome addiction. The ministry provides childcare for children under the age of twelve and serves a meal to all participants. This ministry also serves two prisons located in the area each week. Many who attend these ministries are receiving salvation and becoming part of the local church body. Pastor JD proudly said, "We have some of the most reputable gangsters in this community attending church here and leading some of our ministries. So when people look at them, . . . they go, 'I can't believe this!'" Two of those "notable" people have started a ministry that helps people struggling with issues other than addiction, such as financial management.

When I pressed the group to describe the process for starting and leading ministries at New Life–Barnett, laughter filled the room and David Vernon jokingly said, "Pastor tells us what to do, and we do it!" Then, having thought for a moment, this group of leaders began to speak of an open atmosphere where ideas were encouraged and fostered. Many of the lay leaders spoke not only of feeling they could bring any idea to Pastor JD because they knew he would take it seriously but also of trusting his judgment to let them know if they should move forward or hold off. David Vernon emphasized dialogue with Pastor JD is a vital part of the process of forming any new idea into ministry. He noted how much he had grown by engaging in this kind of process, excitedly declaring he had gone "from leading ministries to leading people that are leading ministries now."

He also described the kind of people who were stepping up into leadership at New Life–Barnett, a description that captures the current atmosphere of this turnaround church: "If you look across our congregation now, there are a lot of people that are what I call unchurched. Or, they spent their first ten years in church and then the next twenty years out of the church. So, these are the type of people that are now getting involved in becoming ministry leaders, and they are on fire for Jesus, and they're going to do whatever they can."

Continuing to talk about the difference in the atmosphere before and after the arrival of Pastor JD, the lay leaders used words like "excitement" and "electric" to describe the current atmosphere. Others spoke joyfully of people "getting saved in our altars." Perhaps the most telling response, however, was from David Cotton: "Do you know the atmosphere between the funerals when somebody is saved, and you know they're saved and they're going to Heaven? It's a completely different atmosphere than somebody that's lost. It's the same thing here."

# CHAPTER 5

# Licking Assembly of God

L icking Assembly of God began in the late 1940s, officially affiliating with the Assemblies of God in 1954. Today,
the church, which meets in a massive building located
on a state route, is highly visible to all entering the small town
of 3,124 residents. That number, however, is a bit deceiving.
Licking is home to a large state penitentiary with nearly fifteen
hundred inmates who are included in the town's population.
The closest urban area, with a population over fifty thousand,
lies 140 miles to the northeast.

One of the only Pentecostal churches in the region, Licking
Assembly experienced rapid growth during its early years.
According to Pastor Paul Richardson, "The church is very rural
and back in the mid-50s was running two hundred to three hundred people in Sunday School." Licking Assembly operated bus
ministries and focused on reaching out to its small community.
However, in the 1960s, a church split occurred causing a large
loss of people. Over three decades and under the leadership of a
single pastor, the church plateaued at twenty to thirty attendees.
In explaining the causes for the stagnation over this extended
period, Pastor Paul identified one cause as competing visions between the pastor and certain influential church members.

In its early years, the church built its sanctuary on a property it owned along a well-travelled road in the community.
As the community grew, however, the state constructed a new

highway, drastically changing the travel patterns of the residents. Essentially, after completion of the new highway, the existing church building became invisible to the community. According to Pastor Paul, if you wanted to find the building, "GPS couldn't help you. It was stuck back in a little neighborhood area." The church deacons pushed for the congregation to build a new building along the new highway, but the pastor did not agree. Instead, he actually led the congregation to build a new but smaller building on the existing church foundation, using materials from the deconstructed church. With that decision, the church deacons and a host of others left to form a new church.

The autocratic leadership style of that long-term pastor was a second cause of the extended decline and plateau. He lacked financial transparency as he and one other church member kept the church checkbook. He refused to allow shared ministry or to utilize deacons or other ministers within the congregation. Instead, the pastor or his wife led all church ministries until their departure.

The pastor elected after their exodus served for ten years. But with no sustainable growth during that period, the pastor resigned. The next pastor elected stayed for one and a half years before the congregation asked him to leave. A succession of interim pastors led the congregation over the next five years. Throughout all this turmoil, Licking Assembly managed to maintain twenty to twenty-five attendees at Sunday worship services. In 2010, the Southern Missouri District Council of the Assemblies of God appointed Pastor Paul Richardson as senior pastor of the church.

Now in his early thirties, Pastor Paul had grown up in a rural Missouri town of fewer than two hundred people. During his childhood, his father served as the pastor of a nondenominational church, even though he was ordained with the Assemblies of God. During Pastor Paul's high school years, he and his family attended an Assemblies of God church in a town of about three thousand people. The church served about 120 attendees and had a good youth group. Pastor Paul felt that church helped him see the positive influence a healthy church can have in a small community. After marrying Julie, Pastor Paul became the youth pastor in a church located in an even smaller town and again saw the impact a well-led church can have in a rural setting.

During the interview process prior to his appointment to Licking Assembly, a female member of the church asked, "Pastor, are you going to stay here for a while or are you going to use us as a stepping stone." Noting the hurt in the member's question and sensing the whole congregation felt that same hurt, Pastor Paul reassured them that if God brought him to the church, he would pour himself out in service to the congregation.

He also sensed a general feeling within the congregation that because they were a small rural church, they were undeserving of a quality pastor. Many pastors had used the church to get experience and then move on because the church, which required a vast amount of work, could not afford to pay a living wage. Even Pastor Paul began his work at Licking Assembly as a bi-vocational pastor, keeping his job as a feed store purchasing agent. He talked about his own temptations and frustrations in regard to this situation through relating a story of presiding over the funeral of a church member one morning and then having to rush home to mow the grass at the church: "This is weird, so weird! This is a weird dynamic of a small church. They entrust me to bury their loved one and minister in time of grief, but they do not value my time enough that someone would come and mow the churchyard in the afternoon." Such moments led him to several conversations with church members to get them to see their need to step up and help.

Although a college graduate, Pastor Paul had no formal seminary training upon accepting the pastorate of the church and had limited pastoral experience: "My world was the business world, and I knew the Bible. Occasionally as a youth pastor, I filled in and preached on weekends at small country churches." In speaking of his attitude coming into Licking Assembly, he stated he had not "come in here thinking, 'All right. This is a turnaround church.' I came in thinking, well, it's a small-town church. And let's see where the Lord can take this." Since becoming the pastor, Pastor Paul has completed a Bachelor of Arts in Christian Management and a Master of Arts in Pastoral Ministry. He is currently working on a Master of Divinity.

His business experience served Pastor Paul well in the early stages of the church's turnaround. In describing the early days of his ministry, he used the words "overwhelming" and "lonely" in part because he "did not have any key leaders" and, not yet having been to seminary, was "learning everything on the fly." (I assured him that even those of us who have attended seminary are still caught unaware of the rigors and requirements of ministry.) At one point, he felt so overwhelmed he contacted a denominational leader: "No one prepared us for this and I don't know where to turn for help," he vented his frustration to the leader. The denominational leader graciously connected Pastor Paul with someone to coach and encourage him in ministry.

Pastor Paul had no trouble formulating and prioritizing the greatest challenges he faced in the early stages of leading the church to turnaround. The first concern was lay leaders. Because most church members were in their sixties and seventies, Pastor Paul and his wife took on the responsibility of leading every ministry of the church: "We had people who were willing to make cookies or show up at events, but because of their age, they weren't as energetic as Julie and I."

However, this aged congregation excelled in hospitality to visitors and made room for new people to take leadership. In describing their receptivity to newcomers, the pastor said,

> *My people loved them [with] wide open arms, which I didn't have to teach them to do because they were just naturally warm and opening and loving. And then I*

*just helped make sure I stewarded that great aspect
of our culture. And so, they've always been good for
new people. They may not always learn their names
right, but when you're 85- to 90-years old, learning
twenty or thirty new names—we give them a pass.
But they have always been warm and welcoming. I
didn't have to teach them that; they already had it.
So, I was able to build upon that friendliness.*

I asked the two lay leaders participating in this study, Larissa Satterfield and Josh Kane, about how the congregation received them when they first attended. Both were in their thirties, were married, had small children, and had come to Licking Assembly after Pastor Paul's appointment. Larissa recounted her spouse had attended the church with his family as a small child but had not been there for many years. Describing the church as "very welcoming," she explained, "I mean, of course, they had gone to church here, and my husband had been that little kid going to church there. So, to see a little church kid come back to church, it was kind of like a homecoming. They were all like, 'Oh, there's little Joey!' I mean, it was like you-never-left kind of thing. They were very welcoming!"

Josh Kane had no prior connection with Licking Assembly except for a friendship with Pastor Paul: "I started coming on Wednesdays. My wife worked on Sunday at a different place. So, we said, 'Let's come on Wednesdays.' The people were very friendly! I'm a little different than they're used to. I like wearing shorts, and I have tattoos, and my ears are gauged and stuff, and I dye my hair quite frequently. So, it was cool showing up like crazy wild in the way I look, but then they were still very much like, 'Hey Josh, how's it going?' So, acceptance of that nature was cool."

As their numbers continued to increase, Licking Assembly purchased and remodeled a larger building to accommodate the now growing congregation. The friendly and welcoming nature of the congregation are evident in the architectural decisions made during this remodel: The foyer is wide open and full of natural light. Couches, tables, and chairs are positioned to facilitate group conversations. Attendees can get a free cup of coffee at the coffee bar. The wall above the coffee bar is adorned with massive vinyl letters reminding people that "no one belongs here more than you!"

The foyer also acts as a casual meeting place throughout the week. Pastor Paul recalled the foyer in the previous smaller building: "In our old church, [fellowship] was very difficult because the old churches were built shotgun style. So, you walk[ed] into a very narrow corridor that opened into the sanctuary. It worked like the cattle chute on a farm: It pushed people through, and it pushed people out, but it didn't facilitate any fellowship. We knew that when we designed a new building, we needed to facilitate the congregation's desire to love on people. And so that's been great!"

The church accomplished their goal of providing a place where people could connect and enjoy one another's company. During a break between interviews, I went into the foyer and found a number of people sitting around drinking coffee. Larissa Satterfield even remarked that new people might feel overwhelmed by how many people greet them, offering them coffee and a snack and starting conversations with them.

A second challenge facing Pastor Paul involved he and his wife's struggle to make ends meet, even though money did not pose a problem for the church. Because the congregants were older and because of good financial stewardship in the past, the church had no problem paying the bills. The congregation was not aware, however, of Pastor Paul's struggle. He explained that the congregation "went from having a retired pastor who owned his own home to a young couple who just left a good job with benefits and stuff moving into the parsonage. My wife and I almost starved our first couple of years. A lot of ministry expenses went on our credit card, such as propane for the parsonage. We went to do hospital visits in our vehicle, and we were out our own gas money."

However, Pastor Paul was quick to take some of the responsibility for this struggle. Licking Assembly was a "District Council" church. As such, the leadership of the Southern Missouri District acted as its local church board. Although Pastor Paul had daily oversight of the administration and direction of the church, other issues, including pastoral salary, property sales, large purchases, and financial accountability, were the domain of the District Council: "Not knowing anything about [church] administration, I didn't know to bring that up. I didn't know how to have honest, open conversations with the Presbyter or to ask him to act on my behalf and work with the congregation. I didn't know those things. And so, for the first few years, I pastored and worked an outside job. [Expenses] went on my credit card and (the Lord has provided since then) but at the time it was very hard."

Pastor Paul had not asked for financial help from the congregation because of the age gap: he and his wife were in their early twenties at that time; the congregation members were mostly in their sixties and seventies and had attended the church longer than Pastor Paul had been alive. He spoke jokingly of how many in the congregation endearingly referred to him as being like one of their "grandkids." He explained that "even though it was an endearment, it's kind of hard to ask a spiritual grandma for extra money when you're a full-grown adult!"

Pastor Paul also explained that no single event shifted the congregational perception of him from grandkid to pastor. Instead, a series of opportunities to lead the congregation into needed change gave him leadership credibility: "Leading gave me the opportunity to say, 'Okay, guys, I love you and you love me. Here's what we need to do!'" He then recounted what he considered his "biggest wins," which happened during the renovation of the old church building prior to purchasing new property: "We had carpet that must have been thirty-five years old, windows were shot out, doors were out; and I led our church to go ahead and renovate that. I used some leadership capital and said, 'Guys, you know we're going to change buildings someday. We know that that's God's will for us, but we got to take care of what we have because people are making decisions every day whether they go to church or not. And we want to make sure we make good impressions.' So, leading through those type of situations helped."

He believed relational leadership was crucial to his ability to make much-needed changes and that personal pastoral care also helped shift the congregation's perspective of him: "Being with families when loved ones passed away, when they were in the hospital, or when they were experiencing situations in their family—shepherding people in those big moments helped established [the perception], 'That's my pastor.' 'That's the guy whom you know was there when I was in surgery.' 'That's the guy who married my grandkids.' 'That's the guy who got my son back in church.' These things helped make that shift between our little kid pastor or preacher."

Pastor Paul keeps a dream notebook in which he writes down the ideas that come to him in prayer before the Lord. He often tells the congregation, "I have dreams in this notebook that you are not ready for—yet." Two dreams in that notebook Pastor Paul believed were top priorities for the church were (a) getting a new building and (b) becoming a sovereign or self-governing church. As of this writing, both of those dreams have been fulfilled.

When asked about the process he uses to bring those dreams to reality, Pastor Paul said he has never had a formal strategic plan. Given the community and church culture, he feels formal "MBA-type" business plans are ineffective with a group of blue-collar people. Instead, the people respond to a "clear vision." They want to understand why a change is needed. The why, for Pastor Paul, is couched in an appeal to a higher cause: "We're building a place for your grandkids to come. A place where your family can worship, be fed spiritually, and a place where people would be nuts not to come to." He stated that once people see the vision and understand the why, they say, "All right, Pastor. Have you heard from God?" When he responds, "Yes," they say, "Well, we know you've done your homework. We don't need to see your notes. Let's go!"

In the first few years of his pastorate, Pastor Paul did not have a local church board to help him make decisions. Instead, he worked with denominational officials to manage the church. Nevertheless, Pastor Paul understood the necessity of engaging congregational stakeholders to get input and advice before making major changes. He quipped that even though he did not have an official board, he did eventually have thirty or forty people to influence toward change. When convinced an idea in the dream notebook needed to become a reality, Pastor Paul began the process by having conversations with key influencers. He described these conversations as "casual." They often occurred during a short road trip the pastor had asked the influencer to take with him. While driving, Pastor Paul would introduce the new idea and ask for input. He repeated this process with other influencers until he believed there was a consensus among them. Then, he would introduce the idea to the larger church and implement it.

Even though the church has grown sufficiently to have an official deacon board in place and multiple unpaid staff members, Pastor Paul still leads through relationship and influence:

> When it comes to big decisions now, it is harder for me to get buy in across 120 people than it was with 20. So, I work to get buy in from the team. I get insight [by asking pastoral staff], "What are the corners that I do not see around? Where are those dark places that I need some clarity on? What are

*we missing on this?" I make sure I do the same with the board. And then when I have my pastoral team and deacon board agree, then I can begin to lead at a congregational level. I think it's important that I still derive the big pictures, but a lot of the other things that would have been a major deal for me four years ago [are] handled between the pastoral staff who's handling it and me.*

As described earlier, when Pastor Paul came to the church, the congregation consisted primarily of elderly men and women. Their adult children and grandchildren no longer lived in the community, moving from the area for work and educational opportunities. Although virtually no children attended the church, Pastor Paul had a dream to minister to children. He asked a minister outside the congregation to come and "plant a children's church just like you would a normal church." He then appealed to the congregation to invite families with kids to be part of this new children's church. Pastor Paul recalled with great joy the impact of what has become a major ministry within the church: "When we started, we saw kids and some young families start coming, and we were like, 'Hey, this could work!'" The growth of the children's ministry became a sign of life for this once dying congregation.

Licking Assembly also makes an intentional effort to be involved in the community it serves. Larissa Satterfield explained how a crazy idea turned into a ministry to youth. At the time, she worked in the public school system and noticed many students did not possess basic life skills or what she called "common sense stuff." Larissa took the idea to Pastor Paul, who was "receptive to the idea" but wanted her to develop it further. The new program evolved into a ministry combining basic life skills like sewing, soap making, and even "how to skin an animal" with a Bible study. It attracted upwards of twenty-five attendees and became the springboard for a "full-blown youth group." In continuing to serve their community over the last eight years, Licking Assembly has also started ministries to single parents, cooked thousands of hot dogs to help support the city's Halloween festivities, formed classes to teach people a variety of skills, and much more.

Josh and Larissa also spoke of how comfortable they felt in taking ideas to Pastor Paul. They trust him not only to help them refine the vision they have for a ministry or outreach but also to tell them no when a ministry idea does not fit the vision or is beyond their current capacity.

Pastor Paul credits a congregation ready for a change as the biggest factor in his ability to lead them: "They loved the church more than I loved the church" and allowed "a couple of twenty-somethings to make changes that would have cost other guys their jobs." Over time, as the church remodeled an older building, replacing pews with chairs and old carpets with new, the style of worship also changed: "They were ready! They had reached the place where they knew that if something didn't change, they didn't have much hope; but they had hope that [my wife and I] were the Lord's anointed for this time and the season. So, they came alongside and helped. It's eight years later, and they love us dearly, and we love them dearly."

He also spoke of a 90-year-old member who had become part of the church in the 1950's. Despite many opportunities to leave, he would not go. The pastor recalled a conversation with this man. As he looked around at the new building the congregation now uses to accommodate their growth, he said to Pastor Paul, "I came into this church in revival, and I believe we're going to leave in revival."

Given the overall age of the congregation, I asked Larissa and Josh why they choose to stay in a congregation where there are virtually no people their age. For Larissa, it was being accepted and needed:

*My father was a pastor, and I was in a church my whole life. But in so many churches it felt like you had to be, like, a certain clique, I guess—I don't mean that meanly—like, to be able to do things, to serve, you had to meet a standard. It wasn't three weeks after we started going Licking Assembly that they needed somebody to clean. I said, "Hey, I live close. I wouldn't mind cleaning the church;" and it was never a question. It was, "We appreciate it. Here's the key!" So, I mean, that sounds silly, but to know that your help was wanted. I mean, they wanted you to be there. So, it was just a different mentality of not having to be at the church for fifty years. You didn't have to be somebody's family. If you were willing to do God's work that they were going to find you a spot that you could be used."*

Josh concurred:

*They are like, "All right, you can do it. We're going to find a place [for you]. We'll figure out how you do it even if it means we have to change the way we do things." For instance, when Larissa took over cleaning, another lady had done it for years, and there wasn't the like, "Well this is my job. You're trying to steal it from me." It's like, "Awesome; somebody else wants to do it." So, it's exciting. Even if a little thing changed, the people got excited about it and it was just cool to see that they were genuine.*

Even with all the changes, new people coming in, and a younger generation taking over leadership, Josh recounted comments he has heard from church members, "This is our home."

"We love this." "We love what the Lord is doing through you and through us. Let's keep going!"

Pastor Paul believes the staying power of the congregation speaks to values learned in rural life, explaining the steadfastness of many members in this way: "They are very committed and loyal. Many of them started a job at what used to be Rawlings Sporting Goods, and they worked there until they retired or [the company] moved overseas. So, they worked lifetimes in a place. They shared life with people. And for them, this was their congregation. They loved it even more than I loved it at the time, and they had poured their lives out here. They raised [their] children here. They did all those type things, and they wanted to see it come back around." Josh Kane painted a similar picture of the congregation's attitude toward change:

> Well, I think just the willingness of the people. I mean, not everybody may have been onboard to begin with, but there was nobody—there was no force— saying, "No, we can't change." It wasn't like it was a big issue, even for the ones that were here that may have not liked that nudge forward. They wouldn't say anything. I mean, not that they didn't feel like they had the right, but they wanted to see it change even though it was hard for them. They wanted to see us move forward. So, they were willing to give it a try even if that change was foreign to them. I guess it's the willingness to let change happen even when it was outside their comfort zone.

In a few short years, this once-dying church received a new pastor, remodeled and sold a church building, purchased a massive building, and began remodeling it. They formed new ministries and grew to 120 attendees on Sunday. Such accomplishments require a large amount of change, which can often produce conflict, especially in an environment of continual and rapid change. Pastor Paul readily admitted he does not like conflict but seems to be dealing with it more now than during the early years of the turnaround. For him, managing conflict is about a personal touch that intentionally seeks to minimize conflict: "By just meeting with someone person to person or by putting an arm around the shoulder Sunday morning and saying, 'Hey, I love you,' or sending a text message saying, 'Hey, so glad you are a part of our church,' it defuses and de-escalates many things on a personal level."

I pushed Pastor Paul to explain what happens if that strategy does not meet the goal of minimizing the conflict. He responded, "Once again I try to de-escalate conflict through relationship and through explaining why and my heart." He cited that any current conflict at Licking Assembly seems to center on miscommunication of the why. As the church has grown from a small group to 120 attendees, new levels of communication have formed. Pastor Paul informs the deacon board and the pastoral staff of the reasons underpinning a decision, but those reasons do not always filter down to the congregation. As a result, people feel left out.

However, most conflict has not been with the congregation but with key leaders with whom the pastor spends much time. Pastor Paul sees these conflicts as issues of proximity rather than of disagreement. During the remodeling project of the new facility, Josh and Larissa (and other church members) volunteered upwards of seventy hours per week for two years to demolish walls, strip floors, build walls, stain doors, and accomplish a hundred other small tasks that formed this large project. The constant togetherness, combined with long hours of physical labor, naturally pushed the limits of relationships between the pastor and volunteers.

Josh and Larissa, however, were quick to change the term "conflict" to "growing pains". They see the relational tension produced by proximity as a natural by-product of being part of a growing church. They also see the hours together as opportunities to learn, grow, and invest themselves in something they believe in wholeheartedly. Pastor Paul and these lay leaders also see growth as a natural source of conflict to manage.

In 2010, Licking Assembly averaged 20 to 25 attendees at Sunday Worship; today, they average 120. Josh Kane joined the church when it numbered 50 attendees. He reckoned that "anytime you have got 70 new personalities coming in, there is conflict." He also praised the pastor's ability to manage the conflict: "So, there may be a little conflict, but Pastor Paul is good at being led by the Holy Spirit. He is a great mediator. I feel like he probably goes home and says, 'Lord why did you give me all these children,' because we are like kids. I mean, sometimes we fuss; but I think at the end of the day, we all come back. We realize we love each other, and we are all after the same thing."

When the church only had a couple of dozen people, a "buddy system" model proved enough to administer the church. Now, at the church's current size, the demand to establish structures and systems to sustain the growth has become paramount. Josh, who works with the children's ministry, spoke of the implementation of helpful systems in light of conflict arising from growth: "We have to do things differently because we're bigger now. For instance, we never had a child check-in system at the old building. We only had two kids and we knew their parents. So, we have a child check-in system now, which we never had to do before." Both lay leaders spoke of the need to plan better and to put events on the calendar because so much is happening in the life of the church. The church is highly involved in community events and outreaches in addition to all the activities of its various ministries. This volume of activity requires coordination of schedules and yearly planning to minimize conflicts.

Pastor Paul discovered an unexpected reality resulting from shifts in leadership: "I think we had people who, when the church was fifty people, were leaders. However, when we got to eighty people, they couldn't handle it. So they left even when we moved over here; we lost people because mostly they couldn't grow to where God was leading the church. They weren't ready for that."

He spoke at length about this unexpected shift and how it changed the way he identified leaders: "When I started, I didn't know who the key leaders were necessarily. So, everybody was an influencer. When there are twenty people, you don't want to get too many of them mad at you. So, at thirty-five or forty people, as I started gaining a little bit of traction, people who were more vocal influenced the church (vocality in a small church is influence; whether it's delegated influence or not, it's an influence). People who are tithing and supporting the church adds to influence." As the church grew from thirty-five attendees to seventy attendees, leadership shifted from vocality and finances to involvement and investment. Although some people still try to influence through vocality, their voices quickly dissipate in the larger crowd.

As new leaders were required, Pastor Paul noticed influence arose from those who were "with me, helping me at the church or helping do projects or doing ministry." With the church growing from 70 to 120 attendees, he became much busier with pastoral care and began keeping office hours. That change created a need for leadership to become more specialized and focused. Instead of one person leading multiple ministries, one or two people were overseeing a single ministry and developing leaders themselves. The church also reached its goal of becoming a self-governing body, requiring the recruitment and training of deacons to assist the pastor. As a result of these shifts, some individuals removed themselves from leadership or turned leadership over to others. Pastor Paul commented on the "weird dynamic" of leadership shifts:

> It's not necessarily all that intentional, but people find comfort levels at different [church] sizes, and

*it shows. Some people are much more comfortable at the 120 level, and they seem to shine. Others shine at 60. When I didn't have people in their forties, thirties, and twenties helping to lead and providing energy, those in their sixties, seventies, and eight-ies did, whether they wanted to or not. Now that the leadership and core workers are much younger, the older ones are like, "You know I don't have to be as involved now. I don't have to do all the work because there's somebody who can do it just as well or do it easier and quicker." So, there's been a lot of shifts in eight years of pastoring. It's a unique situation quite probably.*

Today, Pastor Paul wonders what leadership shifts need to oc-cur to move the church beyond one hundred twenty.

Continuing the vein of leadership, I asked Josh and Larissa to describe the qualities they bring to the church and what qualities they look for when identifying potential leaders. Both mentioned various personal qualities, including tenacity, a willingness to learn, and a love for people. The quality each lay leader saw as most important personally and in others who desire leadership was having "skin in the game." In other words, these lay leaders looked for people who show up, put in the time, and give "100 percent"—people who will make the kind of sacrifices they have made and that Pastor Paul has modeled.

I then challenged Pastor Paul to identify what he might do dif-ferently if he could. He struggled to answer but then spoke about spending more time building relationships and less time griping about "fixing toilets on Sunday morning while wearing a suit." He also spoke of being more intentional about building teams and having a more joyful attitude. However, he had no trouble identifying what he would not change: (a) not blaming the past for everything and (b) being a provider of hope even in the midst of difficulty.

# CHAPTER 6

# New Life Church–Farmington

Navigating to New Life Church–Farmington, formerly known as Pleasant View Assembly of God, was not an easy task; for a time, I thought my GPS wasn't working correctly as I kept going farther and farther into open country. The church has even installed road signs at two junctions to help people find the property.

New Life Church–Farmington sits on a small two-lane road on the outskirts of Farmington, Missouri, a town of approximately eighteen thousand residents. The original church building is a typical red brick structure with a pitched roof. Steep steps lead to a small porch and the entrance. Passing through the glass entry door, one enters a small but very modern foyer, with hardwood floors, a welcome kiosk, fresh paint, and modern lighting, all of which has been recently installed to make members and guests feel more welcome. The sanctuary is a mix of old and new furnishings. The design of the small stage is modern, with a well-lit backdrop of black walls. On the stage sit an electric keyboard, drums, and various stringed instruments. A well-appointed media booth with controls for the projection unit and sound sits at the rear of the sanctuary. The new padded pews and modern lighting create a warm, hospitable atmosphere.

Attached to the red brick building is a massive metal structure built during the tenure of a previous pastor. Originally intended as a new sanctuary, half of this gigantic edifice sits empty today, used only for storing construction equipment. The other half houses a gymnasium, classrooms, and kitchen facilities. Here, the church hosts children's church on Sundays and other youth activities. On weekdays, the local homeschool cooperative uses the gym and some of the classrooms.

Pastor Kevin Kappler began attending New Life Church–Farmington as a high school student in 1985: "I am a prodigy of this church. This church paid for me to get my credentials when I was here. They invested into me." After attending and volunteering at the church for ten years, Pastor Kevin became a full-time associate pastor there, serving in that position for seven years: "I have a lot of history in the church, and those were good years." As an associate, he watched the church grow from seventy attendees to an average of one hundred at Sunday worship. During this season of growth, the senior pastor felt led of the Lord to leave and the church elected another senior pastor. Under this individual's leadership, the church grew to nearly two hundred attendees. At that time, Pastor Kevin felt called to another ministry and left to pursue that calling.

Because the red brick church building was too small to provide enough seating and educational space for the burgeoning congregation, the church began building the metal structure. Soon after the shell of the new building went up, a conflict arose in the congregation that resulted in the pastor's resignation and an interim pastor taking the helm of the church. However, the conflict grew worse, leading to a "couple of church splits." According to Pastor Kevin, over a ten- to eleven-year period, a "large percentage" of people left. Even though the church experienced short seasons of growth, they were soon followed by decline. Still, the church slowly continued the building project.

Christopher Yordy, a lay leader at New Life–Farmington, joined the church in 2003 during a season of stability under a new pastor: "It was a pretty strong church, and we felt comfortable enough to come here," he stated. He reckoned the church was averaging a hundred attendees at that time. Although he spoke highly of the pastoral leadership then, he admitted that, being new, he had been naïve about simmering church problems. He recalled attending a church meeting a year after joining the church where those issues came to light: "There was a business meeting about voting in the pastor again for a certain number of years. He had been here several years and wanted a certain amount of years in his contract. I think the church wanted something different. After a nasty business meaning, [the pastor] walked out. That was the end."

Christopher went on to explain that, after the pastor left, the business meeting continued "like nothing ever happened." One of the deacons raised his hand and put forward a motion concerning the type of songs permissible in worship services, even though the church had a paid minister of music to make those decisions. Christopher raised that point and the motion was defeated. However, the major result of the meeting was that New Life Church–Farmington was again without a senior pastor.

A new interim pastor served the church until the election of a new senior pastor. According to Christopher, the new senior pastor "was very intelligent, but he just did not fit. The church voted him in because the board recommended him, but things just kind of went down from there." Pastor Kevin explained further that this pastor "just didn't gel with the culture of the church." He had come from an urban area and had not successfully adjusted to rural life. Ultimately, he resigned.

The church received another interim pastor and eventually elected another senior pastor. Christopher sadly explained that "pretty much each time [a new pastor] would come, the church kept dwindling." He cited family problems within the church as a major contributor to the turmoil. The church dipped to a Sunday attendance of twenty but grew to fifty attendees under the leadership of yet another pastor who stabilized the church for a time. This pastor proved popular with the people, who showed him great loyalty. When he announced at a church meeting he would be leaving, church members wanted to know where he was going so they could follow him there.

When I asked Christopher why he and his family had stayed during all the conflict and decline, he quickly and emphatically answered, "God put us here! We just stayed. I had no desire to go anywhere else." Although Christopher admitted to having conversations with his wife about leaving, they remained.

The reasons others left the congregation were varied. According to Christopher, "they just got mad and left! Instead of stepping up and trying to help make changes." Other reasons he proffered were disagreeing with something preached or believing other churches had more programs to benefit their families. However, both Christopher and a second lay leader, Jason Finch, pointed to a constant issue of people coming and going, even after the turnaround. According to Jason, the reason for this is consumerism: "People are looking for a different experience with church. I don't know how to describe it other than that. They want something bigger."

In 2013, the Southern Missouri District appointed Pastor Kevin as senior pastor of New Life–Farmington. Although he had served as an associate at the church previously and in other churches for almost twenty years, this was Pastor Kevin's first senior pastorate. Almost immediately after his appointment, a small contingent of people left and started another church in the area. This event proved a small thing compared to what happened only a few months later.

To fund the construction of the metal building, New Life–Farmington had borrowed from a local bank. The loan structure required a certain number of payments and then a balloon payment to settle the note. A few months after taking leadership of the church, Pastor Kevin received notice from the bank that the balloon payment was due. New Life–Farmington did not have the financial resources at that time to keep the commitment they had made with the bank. Pastor Kevin recalled being "aggravated [because]I knew the names of those who signed for the loan, and—nothing against them—but where are these people now to help us with this?"

A representative of the bank met with Pastor Kevin at the church to help him plan for repayment. During the meeting, the pastor asked, "What's the worst thing that can happen?" The representative answered, "The worst that can happen is you might lose the building." Pastor Kevin admitted he did not feel equipped to manage this crisis. In the past, he had worked for ministries large enough to have support staff to handle most administrative tasks. At New Life–Farmington, he was doing almost everything: leading worship and the student ministry, preaching, and managing all the finances. However, he knew he must take a strong leadership stance at this moment if the church was to survive.

The bank agreed to work with New Life–Farmington, mandating that Pastor Kevin prove the church was taking steps to improve its financial position. The bank also required Pastor Kevin to teach the congregation about financial stewardship and to take measures to reduce expenses. At this time, the massive metal building sat empty, its heating bill draining the church treasury. Pastor Kevin took the issue before the church: "I told the church here is the situation with the finances. Here's how we could lose our building. Are you willing to move if we need to move and sell the building?"

The church agreed to place the property up for sale. They listed the building with a realtor, but in ten months only one person showed interest. In the meantime, Pastor Kevin led the church in a plan to restrict access to the metal building, winterize it, and close it down. Impressed by their initial efforts, the bank agreed to allow more time for repayment.

Pastor Kevin also realized the church could not afford to pay his salary. He described his thoughts at this realization in detail: "I remember a few months into it I tell my wife they can't afford to pay us. It wasn't a tremendous amount, but it was a decent salary for this area. I was okay with it. I remember thinking they can't afford to do this. I began to think about what I could do. I thought, 'God, what do I need to do to help this? What can I do?'" Pastor Kevin began looking for employment outside of the church. Because he had grown up in the area, he had contacts and felt he could use those to gain employment.

However, he struggled with the idea of transitioning to bi-vocational, not because he was unwilling but because he believed God wanted him to devote his energy to the church alone. He recounted his prayers at that time: "God, I know you brought us here. I don't understand this. I feel like they need a full-time pastor, but if this is what we have to do to stay, for now, I'll do it. Lord, we just got here! I can't see that You would have us turn and leave!" Pastor Kevin contacted the District leadership, asked for a letter of recommendation, and began searching for jobs.

Shortly after resolving to become a bi-vocational pastor if necessary, Pastor Kevin received a phone call from a former ministry colleague in another state. This colleague wanted to know how things were going in his new position. He jokingly told the colleague, "Things are great! We're about to lose our building, and I am looking for work!" After a few moments, the colleague had to end the call but promised to call back. Sometime later, that ministry colleague called back, offering to send Pastor Kevin a certain dollar amount each month for one year. As the end of that year approached, he would reduce the monthly sum according to New Life–Farmington's ability to contribute to Pastor Kevin's salary. Then another former colleague contacted Pastor Kevin, telling him he would be sending $250 per month for a year. Pastor Kevin was overwhelmed by the events and God's goodness. He informed the church that because of God's intervention, he could restructure his salary package. New Life-Farmington would provide the bulk of Pastor Kevin's salary and funds from the outside sources would make up the difference.

Measures taken by New Life–Farmington to reduce expenses, God's financial intervention, and Pastor Kevin's willingness to sacrifice made it possible to refinance the building loan with the Assemblies of God Credit Union. The pastor proudly noted, "We have never missed a payment!"

Christopher Yordy recalled these crisis moments as opportunities to develop a friendship with Pastor Kevin: "When Pastor Kevin first came, we kind of went around together and spent much time together just doing different things. He would share this and that with me, and I would be like, 'Dude, it will be all right! We've been at twenty-five people, and we're still here.' Just out of nowhere, God miraculously provided. He provided for this church from outside this church."

During this season of financial crisis, Pastor Kevin felt the Lord calling him to challenge the church to begin financially supporting missionaries. Laughing, Pastor Kevin remarked, "I understand it doesn't make sense. I just told the whole church the dilemma we're in financially, and now we're going to spend $50 more each month, but I felt the church trusted me to lead them in that direction." From that moment, the church's financial situation began to improve. Jason Finch supported Pastor Kevin's assertions: "The key to the turnaround in this church, bar none, has been getting involved with missions. That was a key leadership commitment, and the church is blessed because of it."

Supporting missions also led Pastor Kevin and other congregational members to participate in short-term mission trips and helped pave the way for Pastor Kevin to teach the congregation to see their community as a mission field: "If we want to reach people, we have to go where the people are—they are not stopping by our building! It's not a stretch for me to do that. Just do what you do on a regular basis. Go to a gym or a particular restaurant—I am in places about every week. I show my face. I've met so many people."

Pastor Kevin has modeled a lifestyle of what he calls "relational evangelism" and believes it is a key factor in New Life–Farmington's turnaround. Having served as a police chaplain in another state, he took steps to become a police chaplain in his current community. After some initial resistance from the local police department, a door eventually opened. He now serves as chaplain for both the police and the county ambulance service, with ninety employees, and has recently been given an opportunity to teach at the police academy: "I could tell you stories about personally leading people to Jesus in a police car and a city park. I could tell stories of praying with police officers and having a corporate prayer at a police station. It's pretty awesome!"

Pastor Kevin's modeling of evangelism has trickled into the congregational culture. He related this story of a church member who caught the vision of reaching out: "We have cops attending now. Two of them are going to be in our Christmas play as Mary and Joseph, along with their newborn baby playing Jesus. A lady in the church began to see the connection and wanted to do gifts for the police department one year. We did it. The next year, she wanted to do it even bigger, and we ended up going to, like, five municipalities with gifts, which was huge last year. Every time you do those things, you stretch the tentacles of your church farther into other places in the community." Jason told of New Life–Farmington's commitment to praying for each police officer in the community for one year. The church put out a roster with the names of all the officers, and members signed up to pray for the officers individually.

The congregation also reflects the relationship building modeled by Pastor Kevin as they welcome guests into their church. Jason Finch recalled his first visit to New Life–Farmington:

> *I can honestly tell you, my first Sunday, when I came*
> *here about four years ago, I was impressed with how*
> *personable and friendly the people were. Honestly,*

*with some past experiences I've had in church, this hasn't been the case. When you go there as somebody new, you wouldn't have someone to say, "Hi," or shake your hand. Well, that's just kind of how it was. It was not there. At New Life–Farmington, I sensed that personable feeling from the very first Sunday we ever attended. People wanted to do everything to make you feel welcome, and it was a neat thing.*

Furthermore, Jason explained the church's culture of hospitality is vital to the church's vision and is a key ministry.

The culture of hospitality is also vital to handling conflict within the church and among the volunteer staff. Jason stated, "We sit down and work it out. You got to realize there is a greater cause than ourselves. You just got to sit down and work it out together. Then you move on from there. Once it's talked about, it's over; it's in the past. We move on!" He stated Pastor Kevin models that behavior in front of the church. As a result, the church has learned how to handle conflict in a healthy way.

A speaker at a conference Pastor Kevin attended challenged him with this question: "If your church disappeared tomorrow from your community, would the community miss your church?" This question has driven Pastor Kevin to challenge his congregation to move from an inward survival focus to an outward focus. Christopher described the emphasis of the church before Pastor Kevin's arrival: "You know a lot of things we did before him coming were church organized. Always organized around the church family. We would have a thing in the Spring, [a] church barbecue. We would have [a] Fall deal for the church too. I don't remember having any community-oriented events." Now New Life–Farmington is involved in a variety of community events.

Because of Pastor Kevin's connection with the community, another door recently opened. Each year, New Life–Farmington hosts a Light the Night event in a local neighborhood. That year, the church had prepared treat bags and rented bouncy houses and games for the event, but the forecasted weather conditions made them consider canceling. While working out in a local gym, Pastor Kevin heard the owner say he would open his facility to children wanting to trick-or-treat. Pastor Kevin volunteered to bring all the bouncy houses, games, and treats to the gym. He told the owner they would set up tables and do all the work. The event was a huge success and helped New Life–Farmington build credibility in the community.

Christopher proudly spoke of Pastor Kevin's "creative mind," joyfully relaying his thoughts about participating in a recent community parade: "We put the worship band on a float, and I'm, like, you're kidding me. I mean, I am riding on a trailer, sitting down and playing a bass [guitar], thinking, 'I don't even want to look up because I'm not that good.' However, you know, we did that, and how many people came to Sunday service because of that I don't know. But you got to put it out there. You know, you got to try something." Christopher's comments reflect a recurring statement Pastor Kevin makes: "If you don't do something, you might not survive!" For Pastor Kevin, that "something" is anything that may work. He applauds the congregation's attitude toward this experimental way of getting out into the community:

> You know I've heard negative stories from [the] past where pastors tried to do some changes or do something like what we did, but I didn't deal with any of that. People were good about allowing me to make changes and try new things. I tell them thank you from the podium. I tell our seniors, "Thank you for letting us try things. Thank you for letting us do things that maybe you wouldn't care about as much." We had a handful of senior adults, and I have to give kudos to those people. They were fantastic to let us

*try things. I presented ideas to the church, like, if this doesn't work, well, we'll just quit doing it. We need to try something. We tried it and they were fantastic!*

This "trying something" also meant changing the name of the church. Pastor Kevin presented the idea of a name change to the members of what was then Pleasant View Assembly of God and explained his thinking. He believed a new name would reflect the new outward focus of the church and its multigenerational congregation. Pastor Kevin had heard from people outside the church that the old name was reminiscent of a retirement home. The name change was put to the vote and unanimously passed. A local lawyer agreed to help the church pro bono; and, after a year of "aggravation," the church name was officially changed to New Life–Farmington.

Christopher described the church's attitude about this change as positive, something that "energized the people": "I have seen the name change of the church. A lot of folks might look at that and say it's just a cosmetic change. I think when we changed the name of the church, it changed people's attitudes. It showed that there was something fresh and something new." He believes the congregational attitude toward change is a direct result of Pastor Kevin's leadership style: "Pastor Kevin is a very positive person. He's positive about how he approaches situations with people. I think that has helped a lot. I think because of him being a very personable person to approach—you know, Pastor Kevin has a good heart. No job is too small for him at the church. It takes everyone working together to make everything work the best way. And I think that's been something that he has really been able to communicate to everyone."

In sharing his process for communicating change to the congregation, Pastor Kevin emphasized the need to build relationships with congregants before making significant changes: "Let the people know who you are outside of the pulpit; build strong ties with your people. And as much as you can, let them know your heartbeat beside just being the guy behind the pulpit. It's amazing how people will be gracious and forgiving if they know who you are outside of just the preacher." He then explained how he utilizes those relationships to cast vision in the church: "I think vision is conveyed by constant repetition. When I present an idea to the congregation, I always try to present things with excitement: this is what we're going to be doing, we're going to try this, we're going do this, we're going to have this, and we're going to try and do this. The major changes like the name change are brought to a meeting and we vote, but you cast that vision to them first. You help them see the value of the change." For Pastor Kevin, value refers to the higher purpose for the change.

In recounting the process of getting the church foyer updated, Pastor Kevin gave a clearer picture of how he works with the church to effect change. First, he takes the idea to his newly formed deacon board. The deacons at New Life–Farmington view their role as pastoral support. Christopher serves on the deacon board and gave a fuller explanation of their function: "Our role is to be supportive of the pastor. He's the leader of the church. You know, to me, it's not, 'No, pastor, you can't do this! No, pastor, you can't do that.' I mean, he's got to be a leader of the church. I know there's a balance. Honestly, he's the leader of the church, and he is ultimately responsible. We are there to support him."

Pastor Kevin clarified he does not go to the deacon board for permission but for input. He views his relationship with the deacons as collaborative. They help him clarify vision and identify potential obstacles in moving forward. He also admitted when he and the deacons can't reach consensus, he steps back and reconsiders the idea. However, if he is confident the Lord has directed him toward a certain goal, a lack of consensus may not stop him from continuing.

After filtering the idea of updating the foyer through the deacon board, Pastor Kevin sent letters to the church members stating the higher reason for the needed update: "This is the first thing people see when they walk into the church, and I want them to see we care." Then he appealed for financial help from members. He kept the vision for an updated foyer in front of the people by receiving a "miracle offering" each month for a few months. God miraculously provided money for the update through an outside source desiring to help New Life–Farmington, and the project was completed.

Knowing the limits of his abilities in certain areas, such as construction, Pastor Kevin also goes to individuals in the congregation who possess skills in the trades for advice. He walks them through the idea, asks for input, and asks questions. Sometimes the people he consults aren't sure his ideas are good. For instance, the decision to paint the stage walls black raised the question, "Why black?" This question was one more of curiosity than of fear of change. Pastor Kevin explained black helps hide wires and cables used during dramas and other productions New Life–Farmington puts on each year, and the congregation trusted him to make the decision.

I specifically asked the lay leaders how the congregation felt about the changes Pastor Kevin had brought to the church. Jason Finch's response indicates the church has been quite receptive to the changes: "You know, I have not heard anyone say anything negative about any change that we have made. It's like one of those things: This is the change, and this is the direction we are going. In the years I have been here, I don't think I have heard anyone say anything negative about any change we've made." He added that a small minority may have felt left out of the decision process. However, in talking with those members, he was able to clear up misperceptions they had and maintain the relationships he had with them.

As of this writing, New Life–Farmington has grown from 40 attendees in Sunday worship in 2013 to 102. Most of that growth has occurred in the last three years. The church has begun new ministries and reformed and relaunched existing ministries. The once closed gymnasium half of the metal building is now open, and both the gym and the brilliantly decorated rooms for youth and children's ministries are actively used.

Christopher Yordy remarked that 75 to 80 percent of the church attended a recent dinner to celebrate the contribution of volunteers. Where once very few people were involved in anything at New Life–Farmington, now people are stepping up. Christopher believes the catalyst for the increased involvement is that they see how God is working and want to be part of the action. Jason Finch credited new or reshaped ministries for the increased involvement. He spoke specifically about the ministries to children and youth: "If the kids come, the parents will come." This axiom has proven true for New Life–Farmington; and with that increase in children and youth, new volunteers have stepped up to help. Both lay leaders readily attributed the greater participation of members in ministry to Pastor Kevin's leadership.

In terms of getting members involved, both lay leaders repeatedly said, "Pastor Kevin is not afraid to ask!" They made no mention of a formal process for members to discover their gifts and talents, although a rarely used form is available for members to express interest in volunteering in certain ministries. Instead, Pastor Kevin looks for places to get people involved and asks them to serve. Christopher elaborated: "Unless you're asked, most people assume things are getting done. I am sure it can't be easy for Pastor Kevin to ask people to do things. I know it's hard for me to ask people for something. There are all different personalities in the church, but you have to be the type of person that says, 'Can you help me out.' I think that if Pastor Kevin is asking me to help [it's] because there is a real need. But getting people to do one thing gets them involved, then they buy in."

Once someone agrees to serve, the appropriate ministry leader trains and mentors that person in the ministry area. Ministry leaders are expected to build ministry teams. To avoid burnout and to ensure volunteers participate in Sunday worship, volunteers share ministry. Depending on the size of the team, a member may serve one or two times per month, as Jason Finch explained: "When people get stuck doing the same task every Sunday, they eventually only come to church to do their job."

When asked to identify the greatest challenges and victories in turning the church around, Pastor Kevin and Jason Finch both spoke of being a little frustrated with the seemingly slow progress of growth. Christopher saw the slow growth a result of realistic expectations. All identified the greatest challenge faced by the church as the coming and going of people during the first few years of the turnaround. Still, Jason and Christopher spoke positively about the whole turnaround process, seeing their involvement in the process as an opportunity for personal growth and maturity.

Pastor Kevin focused on the victories: financial miracles, renovations, the willingness of the congregation to trust him, and the name change. He struggled, however, to identify a single defining moment when he knew the church would survive. Instead, he pointed to a whole host of little moments that led to bigger moments. In terms of doing something differently, he acknowledged that he might handle some people leaving differently. However, given the same circumstances, he'd do things the same way.

# CHAPTER 7

# Communication and Conflict

C oming into their senior pastorates, the three pastors highlighted here each faced a church in crisis. Handling these crises effectively allowed these men to build trust with their new congregations, identify lay leadership, and move their churches forward to accomplish the visions set before them. In dealing with various crises, these pastors had to communicate change and to manage conflict effectively. They also realized pastors cannot do everything themselves. They must work together with their lay leaders and congregants to move their churches forward.

## Communication

Before change can occur, people need to know what has to change and how it must change. That requires clear communication on the part of leadership. Pastors Paul Richardson and Kevin Kappler prefer a relational approach to communicating change to their lay leaders and church members. For Pastor Kevin, this means letting his people know him as a person, not just as a pastor: "It's amazing how people will be gracious and forgiving if they know who you are outside of just the preacher." He also believes it's important to "cast the vision repeatedly to them first" before attempting any significant change so they will see "the value of the change"; in other words, how does that change reflect the vision cast for the church, how does it help the church "better serve its community"?

Pastor Paul keeps a "dream notebook" in which he writes down his ideas from his prayer time with the Lord. He also feels presenting a "clear vision" to the church is essential so his congregants understand why they need to change things and why the recommended change fits the vision. When they see the vision and understand the why behind the needed change, they are ready to begin working toward that change.

Pastor JD relies heavily on his corporate experience to communicate a vision for change. He read and used *Managing Transitions: Making the Most of Change* by William Bridges[70] in "managing some very large transitions in the business world." He has applied those techniques in communicating change with his church: "First, you must identify the issue. What do you need to change? Then you have to sell people, show people, and convince or compel them to see that that change is needed. Typically, when you equip people with the data or information of what needs to be done, they will end up making the same decision you're trying to get them to go to. And so, instead of manipulating people you are equipping them to make good decisions."

Both Pastors Paul and Kevin led their churches initially without the help of local church boards. Pastor Paul relayed the necessity of "engaging congregational stakeholders to get input and advice" and communicating with people within the congregation who could "influence toward change" in the absence of a formal board of deacons. Both churches now have deacon boards, and both pastors engage with them regularly for input and advice concerning changes in their churches. For Pastor Kevin, "a lack of consensus" with the deacons at New Life–Farmington "causes him to step back and reconsider an idea"; but it does not "prevent

---

70 Bridges, 2017.

him from moving ahead" when he is "confident the Lord [has] directed him toward a certain goal."

Pastor Paul works relationally with his deacon board as well. As Licking Assembly of God has grown, he understands that "when it comes to big decisions now, it is harder for me to get buy in across 120 people." He relies on getting "buy in from the team," which includes his pastoral staff and board of deacons. When the two groups agree, he knows he can "begin to lead at the congregational level."

## Conflict

Regardless of the amount of buy in a pastor may garner from pastoral staff, deacons, lay leaders, and congregants, conflict is bound to arise. As Pastor JD said, conflict is "a necessary means to an end." For him, the "let's agree to disagree" mentality does not really deal with the issue at hand; "get[ting] into it and "figur[ing] it out" allows for real give and take: "They're probably going to change me some, change themselves some, and so, I'm not afraid of that." He emphasizes that "as a leader, you can't be afraid of conflict." However, he also believes once a decision is made, "you stick with it no matter how tough it gets."

Pastor Kevin also insists conflict is a natural by-product of change. He counts on communicating the vision and the need for certain changes clearly and repeatedly to his congregation to mitigate such conflict. The idea seems to be that repeated exposure to an idea softens people's resistance to a change. But Pastor Kevin also believes the positive effects created from smaller changes increases the congregation's trust in him, making major changes easier. Implementing smaller changes early on also helps pastors "test the waters" for future change.

Pastor Paul readily admits his disdain for conflict yet seems to be dealing with it now more than in the early years of the turnaround. He continues to rely on personal interactions (e.g., a one-on-one meeting, an "arm around the shoulder," an "I love you") to minimize conflict. If those actions don't resolve the problem, Pastor Paul continues his relational approach, adding an explanation of the "why and the heart" of the change. He feels most of the conflict currently in his church centers on the miscommunication of the "why," noting sometimes the deacons and pastoral staff do not always communicate effectively with the congregation, making church members feel left out of the change process. He also feels that in his situation conflict with key leaders is related to proximity more than to disagreement over specific changes or ideas, as shown in their purchase and remodeling of a building: the fast growth of the church required more space to accommodate attendees, which led to the purchase of a large building once used for retail space and a two-year re-modeling project conducted by volunteers from the church and community. The constant togetherness, coupled with the long hours of physical labor, naturally pushed the limits of the pastor-volunteer relationship.

In commenting about this proximity conflict, Josh Kane from Licking Assembly interestingly refused to use the word *conflict*. Instead, he referred to these relational tensions as "growing pains" that are a natural part of church growth. Both lay leaders from that church had spent upwards of seventy hours a week dur-ing the remodeling of the new church building and saw this time together as an opportunity to learn, grow, and invest themselves in something they believe in wholeheartedly. Larissa Satterfield, from Licking Assembly, believed conflict emerges in their grow-ing church from two primary areas: (a) the administration of growing numbers of ministries formed to reach people for Christ and (b) the rapidity of role change requiring leaders to work out-side their "comfort zones." Both Josh and Larissa praised Pastor Paul's ability to manage conflict because he is "good at being led by the Holy Spirit" and "is a great mediator." From time to time, pastors must also deal directly with an individual who foments conflict within the congregation. Pastor JD described one such individual as a "constant thorn." Given his straightforward approach to leadership, the pastor called this person and his wife into his office and forthrightly told the man his comments were undermining the church's vision. He needed either to stop or to leave the church. After his wife encouraged her husband to abandon his ill will against the pastor, he repented and became an avid supporter.

When I came to Life Point Church, it was easy to see the big changes ahead of us. I knew that making those big changes immediately would be a recipe for disaster. I did not have the trust of the people. I had been appointed, not elected, as the lead pastor. The congregation was hurting and tired of hearing about vision and change—they had heard it all before. I recognized that my very presence was the biggest change they could handle for a while. So instead of jumping into remodeling and restructuring, I was just present. My office door was open. I spent time with whoever gave me the opportunity. I met with leaders to hear their stories and get a sense for their ministry passion. I learned a lot about the history of the church. As a result, I began to see the potential personality and leadership conflicts that lay ahead of me as bigger changes were implemented. And, more importantly, I began to see those church members who were going to take the ride of change with me.

As a leadership coach, I've heard story after story from pastors petrified of conflict. That fear of confrontation keeps them on edge emotionally, ultimately hindering the growth of the church. One excuse I often hear for not confronting divisive church members goes like this: "If I confront the person, he or she will leave the church." Well, they might. But that may also be a good thing. One of the best days in Life Point's turnaround happened when a large group of people decided to leave. Their bullying behavior held hostage those people who desired to rebuild a caring and hospitable church.

Unfortunately, former members can continue to be thorns in the side of churches during the turnaround process. One former member of Life Point chose to publicly embarrass me at the local bank. As I stood at the teller's counter attempting to deposit my paycheck, this person, who had caused trouble at the church for years, decided it was his chance to voice his anger that I was being paid at all. In the lobby of that bank, he announced what he thought was my salary (he grossly overestimated it), accused me of being a "money loving preacher," and let me know he wasn't going to stand for it. I was so startled by his viciousness I could not answer him. In retrospect, I am sure the Holy Spirit was restraining my voice. Later, after I had cooled off, I went to the man and confronted him about his actions. But the public damage was done. The long-standing reputation of our church as a conflict-filled church had been confirmed in the minds of all those standing in the bank that day.

Revitalizing a dying church requires strong leadership. To lead well requires pastors to confront these kinds of people when necessary. Instead of confronting them, however, many pastors internalize their emotions and live in constant mental turmoil all in the name of humility. Pastoral burnout, in my experience, doesn't always happen because of a few bad decisions or leadership missteps. It happens because leaders are controlled by fear and refuse to confront divisive people. As a result, their families suffer, their churches suffer, and the communities they are called to serve suffer. In the end, pastors allow Satan to distract them from the vision God has placed in their hearts.

The Apostle Peter reminds all believers, "Be alert and of sober mind. Your enemy the devil prowls around like a roaring lion looking for someone to devour."[71] Every preacher has reminded their congregations of Peters metaphoric description an enemy who bellows loudly but has no real power. The noise of the lion

---

71 1 Peter 5:8 (NIV)

is simply a scare tactic meant to rattle the mind of the believer and distract him or her from the remembering the power of God working in them. When my family and I lived in South Africa we were fortunate to visit numerous game parks and see lions in their natural habitat. I have vivid memories of being awakened by the roaring of lions as the sun came up. The voluminous low bass tones of the lion's roar reverberated in my chest. It startled my family from sleep and set us all on edge for a few moments. We relaxed after remembering we were safely tucked in our room and surround by high-voltage fencing. There are people in the church used by Satan to roar and rattle. Those who create conflict and chaos for what they believe are good reasons.

I remember walking into Sunday worship at Life Point Church thinking, "Who's going to be the lion today? Who will be the one who comes with petty complaints or to once again compare me to another preacher from days gone by!" At first, I let those voices rattle me to the point of paralysis. I agonized over simple decisions that should have been easy for even inexperienced leaders to make. Then after I made those decisions, I spent days second guessing myself. I walked around for months with knots in my stomach. One desperate day, I fell on my face at the altar in the church auditorium. I poured my heart and soul out to God for what seemed like hours. Somewhere in my lament the Holy Spirit surrounded me with peace. It was then I remembered God's call to revitalize this church came complete with God's grace to accomplish His will. Suddenly the lion's roar diminished in my ears. Yes, there were several more months of "well-intentioned" church members pointing out my inadequacies. But somehow their voices didn't carry the same weight. Through the comfort of the Holy Spirit I was able to move forward and experience God's grace in a new way.

Don't misunderstand. Strong leadership is not an excuse for unkind or unchristian behavior or a reason to boot out everyone who resists change. It is the responsibility of a good shepherd to hear what people are saying and take their concerns seriously. However, as church leaders, we get to choose the level of frustration we are willing to tolerate. When pastors refuse to confront—and hide from—conflict, they are telling their congregations that God's mission is secondary to the agenda of a few dragons. And, ultimately, failure to deal with the dragons teaches the church how to treat leadership.

# CHAPTER 8

# Facing Challenges Head On

In turning around their churches, these three pastors have had to deal with a variety of specific challenges. Although each church is unique, they have faced several common issues in the areas of finance, culture, leadership, and hospitality.

**Finances**

Each pastor had to deal with major financial problems soon after accepting the call to the senior pastorate at his church. In addition, both Pastors JD and Kevin were unaware of the extent of the financial crises their churches faced when they accepted their calls. This seems to be a recurring problem with pastors I coach. Rural churches tend to attract inexperienced pastors who think asking to see the church financials is off-limits or may hurt their chances of being hired. The reality is that some pastoral candidates are simply looking for a stepping-stone to help them get experience. Sometimes the pastoral search committee paints a rosier picture of the church's financial position (and attendance numbers), believing it will attract better qualified pastoral candidates. Either way, transparency about church finances seems rare. But as I interviewed these turnaround pastors, I found the answer to solving their church's financial problems was honesty with the congregation and decisive action.

At New Life–Barnett, a declining membership hindered the church's ability to meets its financial obligations. Exacerbating this was a huge church building designed to accommodate a once growing congregation that now drained the church of its monetary resources. The church owed nearly $10,000 in back payments to various vendors and companies. Pastor JD approached the problem through prayer, noting his congregants were "giving people but they were tapped out of resources . . . we just really had to pray that God would do something miraculous and He did." Not only was the church able to work out a payment plan with the gas company, but a young couple also tithed on a settlement they had received from a car accident. This "allowed [the church] to . . . go forward." The pastor also closed off half of the building his first year at the church, reducing expenses by approximately $4,000. Further easing the church's financial problems was a donation from this bi-vocational pastor's other employer.

Pastor Kevin found himself faced with a balloon note due on the loan for the construction of a new church building and gymnasium, a commitment made prior to his tenure at the church. Not having the money to repay the loan, the pastor contacted the bank and then explained the situation to the church. The congregation agreed to sell the new building. In the meantime, Pastor Kevin led the church in a plan restricting access to the gymnasium and unfinished sanctuary to stop the financial drain on church resources from heating and upkeep of those areas. Impressed by their initial efforts to stem their financial problems, the bank agreed to allow more time for repayment.

Both Pastors JD and Kevin worked with their congregations to improve their financial positions long term. Pastor JD led church leaders through a budgeting process and created a six-month cash reserve. The bank holding the mortgage to New Life–Farmington actually mandated Pastor Kevin teach the congregation about financial stewardship. Pastor JD refrained from receiving a salary from the church for the first three years of his leadership and petitioned the Southern Missouri District to let New Life–Barnett keep 100 percent of his ministerial tithe to help get through the financial crisis.

When Pastor Kevin understood the church could not really afford to pay him, he prayed, asking for guidance. He contemplated working a second job; but before securing a position, he received promises from two colleagues to send him monetary donations each month for a predetermined period. As the church's finances improved, the amount of those donations decreased. As a result, Pastor Kevin restructured his salary until the financial position improved.

Even in those financially difficult times, Pastor Kevin felt the Holy Spirit prompting him to challenge the church to give to global missions. Shortly after informing the church body of its financial crisis with the mortgage, Pastor Kevin felt led to ask his church to commit an additional $50 each month to support missionaries. He admitted his action did not seem to make sense, but he believed God had impressed this need on his heart. From the moment the church agreed, their financial situation improved. As Chris Yordy commented, "The key to the turnaround in this church, bar none, has been getting involved with missions."

In contrast, Licking Assembly did not experience the same kind of financial difficulties and problems. Instead, Pastor Paul's lack of understanding concerning how to deal with denominational leadership about his salary created financial problems for him. The church, itself, had a firm financial foundation due to good financial stewardship on the part of its older congregation. However, church members were used to having "a retired pastor who owned his own home" and were unaware of the difficulties the new young pastor and his wife were having. Because the church board consisted of denominational officials, to get a salary increase, the pastor had to petition the denomination for help. Not knowing how to do this, Pastor Paul and his wife charged many expenses on their credit card that should have been paid by the church, including "propane for the parsonage." This lack of knowledge made it necessary for Pastor Paul to work an outside job.

When I arrived at Life Point Church, the cash financial position was relatively good. Not having a full-time pastor for some time had allowed them to build a healthy cash reserve. We also received a grant from the Southern Missouri District to help the church pay my salary and do some much-needed maintenance on the buildings. However, the church was in deep debt in relation to its membership numbers. Prior to my coming, church leaders had renegotiated the church mortgage terms to reduce the monthly payments. This ensured the current budget could cover the other regular bills, but the income was still declining. The church building was in disrepair and in dire need of updating. If Life Point was going to welcome new people and create an atmosphere of hospitality, we needed a clean, modern, and attractive space. The money we had on hand was not enough to pay the bills we owed and simultaneously fund the ministry we needed to do; God was at work to help us.

Another larger Assemblies of God church near us had a men's ministry that helped churches do construction projects. When I approached the pastor to ask for help, he readily agreed to send a team. Our agreement was simple: they provided the labor and Life Point purchased the materials. The team arrived on a Monday morning and worked and worked and worked. They tore up flooring, stripped wallpaper, repaired cracks, laid porcelain tile, installed new light fixtures, painted walls, and so much more. Over a five-day span, this team invested four hundred man-hours into remodeling the building. At the end of the week, I went to the pastor to get the receipts for materials. He looked at me and said, "What receipts?" I said, "For the tiles and paint and such." He looked at me and said, "Pastor Danny, someone on the team has decided to pay for all the materials, so don't worry about it!" I was stunned and awed by the display of generosity and love for our little church. That was only the beginning of multiple financial miracles God performed in our congregation over the last six years.

In 2016, I felt led by the Holy Spirit to challenge Life Point to become debt free. It was time to retire about $40,000 in mortgage debt. At our annual meeting, I cast a vision for retiring the debt and the people responded. I believed God would help us be debt free in twelve months not because we couldn't pay the mortgage but because it was time to use that money for more important matters of ministry. God was calling our church to reach out to middle school students, and we needed money to make that happen. No one gave huge amounts of money. Most of our folks just didn't have large sums to give. Instead, a majority gave something faithfully every month to meet the need. And although we did not reach our twelve-month goal, we did succeed in eighteen months. We burned the mortgage (symbolically) and diverted that money toward launching our youth ministry.

I have never let money be an obstacle to the mission of God, nor have I maintained a reckless attitude toward financial stewardship. After the exodus of several families, I took a drastic reduction in salary and began teaching at SUM Bible College and Theological Seminary. I also eliminated a paid administrative position, a hard but necessary decision. Delivering the news to the employee nearly gave me a heart attack. But it had to be done. If the church was going to survive, I could not sit idly by. I had to act, and I did. However, I have never stopped praying for and expecting God to come through. I can bear witness to this fact: He has never failed. Sometimes, He answered by giving us creative ideas to do effective ministry on a shoestring budget. Other times, an unexpected offering came in from a church member or interested outside party. I have also never been shy about asking the congregation to step up and fund the mission of God. Way too many pastors fear reprisal from church members if they dare speak about money. My suggestion: get over the fear, trust God, and ask!

## Culture

All three pastors related the need to change various cultural aspects of their respective churches. At New Life–Barnett, major cultural challenges involved two aspects of public worship: the use of spiritual gifts and the music used during services. Assemblies of God churches are both Pentecostal and Evangelical, believing in and encouraging supernatural manifestations of the Holy Spirit. These manifestations include speaking in an unknown tongue, the interpretation of tongues' speech, verbal messages of wisdom and knowledge, and public prophetic utterances. [72] Assemblies of God churches believe these supernatural gifts work to build up God's people when properly exercised. In addressing some of the abuses of supernatural gifts in the Corinthian church, Paul instructs the church to allow these gifts, "but everything should be done in a fitting and orderly way."[73]

At New Life–Barnett, however, the alleged exercise of these gifts brought chaos rather than edification. Pastor JD viewed this situation as a hindrance to church growth that needed to be corrected and aligned with biblical instruction and church vision. He confronted this problem with love and firm conviction, even though some members believed he was "stifling the Spirit." Keeping the vision of connecting people to Jesus at the forefront, he challenged people to change their paradigm about spiritual gifts and lovingly confronted members whose actions brought confusion to the congregation during worship. He set a new expectation of order, allowing for biblical instruction in the exercise of spiritual gifts while keeping in mind the lack of familiarity new people might have with these practices.

---

72 See Acts 2, 10, and 19 and 1 Cor 12–15 for speaking in an unknown tongue; see 1 Cor 14:27 for the interpretation of tongues' speech; see 1 Cor 12:8 for verbal messages of wisdom and knowledge; see 1 Cor 12:10 for public prophetic utterances.

73 1 Cor 14:40 (NIV).

Although music styles vary from church to church, emotional and heartfelt singing and music are vital to the life of Assemblies of God and Pentecostal churches. At New Life–Barnett, the music and vocals seemed lackluster, the pastor noting some of the "people on the worship team . . . couldn't sing . . . it wasn't their gifting." He approached this challenge directly, again with love and through an appeal to a higher cause. He also remained resolute in keeping the vision of excellence, which he believed helped create an atmosphere of "self-selection" as people realized their talents lay in other areas of service. This minimized confrontation and conflict. Ultimately, the music ministry developed a procedure for auditions and a set of expectations team members must agree to follow.

For Pastor Paul, the greatest cultural challenge was the age gap between most of the members of the church and the new pastor and his wife. The congregants were mostly in their sixties and seventies; the pastor and his wife were in their twenties. Because of this huge age gap, the couple found themselves taking responsibility for leading every ministry of the church because, although "willing to make cookies or show up at events," the members simply "weren't as energetic" as the he and his wife. Many of the congregants even endearingly referred to him as one of their "grandkids." This mindset changed slowly over time through a series of opportunities to lead the church through smaller, incremental changes. Pastor Paul also credited his interactions with the congregation through pastoral care opportunities in shifting their impression of him from grandchild to pastor. His "shepherding" when families suffered the loss of a loved one, were ill, or were simply facing unexpected or difficult circumstances established Pastor Paul as their pastor.

Connected to this age gap was the perception that small rural churches deserve below average pastors. Because these churches often cannot afford to pay salaries commensurate with the enormous amount of work required, many pastors use their positions in such churches as steppingstones to larger congregations. Pastor Paul also started to feel this same temptation because of frustration over having no staff and few key leaders to handle some of the myriad tasks for which he was responsible. However, he again approached the problem relationally, engaging in several conversations with members about stepping up and taking ownership of some of the tasks. He also noted feeling overwhelmed because he was having to "learn everything on the fly" and contacted one of the denominational leaders for help. This person then connected him with someone to mentor and encourage him.

The most consistent cultural change experienced by all participating churches was their redirection from an inward focus of maintenance and survival to an outward focus of outreach and missions. Each church moved at a different pace, but all eventually established ministries focused on serving the communities around them, including children's and youth ministries, ministries for those suffering from drug and alcohol addictions, prison ministries, chaplaincies, and cooperative enterprises with other community organizations.

At New Life–Barnett, all the lay leaders interviewed agreed this change of attitude toward ministry was key to their church's turnaround. Instead of a few individuals leading everything, the goal became leader multiplication. Again, Pastor JD approached this challenge to the culture relationally, working with lay leaders to understand they were "stealing opportunities from everyone else" by trying to do everything themselves. He also appealed to a higher cause, working with lay leaders to build a culture of replication and releasing of ministry in insisting lay leaders always train replacements for the sake of ministry continuation.

New Life–Barnett developed several ministries as they moved their focus outward. Their youth ministry provided meals for all participants each Wednesday night. The church serves an impoverished community, with "a lot of drugs and a lot of alcoholism" and people living "on disability or off the government." Several lay leaders pioneered a biblically-based recovery ministry for adults, providing childcare and also serving meals to all participants. Volunteers conducted a prison ministry twice a week, bringing many of those who attended to salvation and assimilation in their local church. An offshoot of this ministry was a financial management program for those struggling with money problems.

The congregation at Licking Assembly consisted primarily of senior men and women whose children were adults. Children were virtually lacking in attendance. Pastor Paul's dream was to build a children's ministry. After presenting his vision to the congregation, he invited a minister outside the congregation to "plant a children's church." The pastor also encouraged members to invite families with children to participate in this new venture. Through this ministry, young families started coming, breathing new life into the church body.

Licking Assembly also began a youth program in a rather unconventional way: providing classes in life skills combined with Bible study. Students learned things not normally taught in the public-school system (e.g., sewing, soap making, animal skinning). As the program grew, it developed into a "full-blown youth group." By providing ministries such as those for single parents, increasing their involvement in community events like the Halloween festivities, and forming community classes, the church firmly established itself as a positive stakeholder in the community.

Pastor Kevin also encouraged his congregation to reach new audiences for Christ by participating as a church in community activities: "If we want to reach people, we have to go where the people are." He modeled this through "relational evangelism." His previous experience as a police chaplain led him to pursue doing so in his current community. This ministry grew to include the police department, the county ambulance service, and the police academy. As church members caught his vision for this ministry, they added to it. As a church, they provided gifts for police officers, starting with their community and growing to include five municipalities. Members also committed individually to praying for a specific officer for one year. In addition, the church increased its visibility through participating in community events such as parades.

About three years into our turnaround at Life Point, Vicki, one of our members, asked to meet with me to talk. A few days later, we met in the newly renovated lobby of our church. I didn't know exactly what she wanted to talk about but knew she had a heart for people. Vicki opened the conversation and just began pouring out her heart about making a difference for others in our town. Tears filled her eyes as she shared her dreams of finding ways to serve others. I thought to myself, "Can this be true?" Let's face it, pastors don't get these kinds of conversations very often. Vicki and I began to brainstorm ways to make her dreams a reality. Over the past few years, God has given Vicki and me opportunities to minister to people in Odessa. More importantly, God has shown our little church the massive need that exists in our rural community, especially among our school-aged children.

Although Life Point Church had done some community events, honestly, they had not gone very well. Our heart was in the right place, but we had made a fatal assumption: somehow we had convinced ourselves we knew what the community needed. We were wrong. During the conversation in the lobby with Vicki, a thought came to mind: what if instead of assuming we know what the community needs, we simply begin asking community stakeholders what they need? We tried it. It worked!

Our leadership team decided the most logical place to help meet needs was in our local school system. We went to the superintindent of schools and asked, "What do you need." Trust me, he knew the needs of his student population. It's been Life Point's privilege to help with a host of projects and to know we are meeting real needs. One year, we provided winter outerwear for elementary students. In just a few weeks after the need was presented to the church, members had purchased and donated more than a hundred new coats, pairs of gloves, and winter caps. It was a joy to show up at the school offices and deliver those coats. Another year, the school system explained a number of elementary students did not have adequate under garments. Again, the church sprang into action. We put up a huge sign shaped like a pair of boxer shorts with the words, "Drop your drawers here." Below the sign was a shelving unit where donations could be placed. In total, we gathered six hundred pairs of underwear.

Recently, Life Point received a generous donation of about two hundred hygiene kits from Convoy of Hope–Rural Compassion. These kits contained soap, razors, feminine items, and more. We wondered what we might do with this many kits, but God was at work. When I called the school to ask if they had any use for such items, the school nurse was elated. The school had just decided to start a "shower program." For some students, access to a hot shower was not a reality. They showed up at school without having bathed and were being ridiculed and bullied by unkind and uncaring students. This program would allow them access to showers before school. The hygiene kits could not have come at a better time. The school needed soap, combs, and razors—basically everything in the donated kits. They also needed towels and washclothes. We sent out a text to the members of Life Point and they responded with generosity. In less than twenty-four hours, members had purchased and donated a few dozen towels and washcloths. Again, a sense of joy and fulfillment washed over Vicki and me as we delivered the first round of towels and hygience kits. Since then, Vicki has continued to work with the school nurse to resupply the kits as the need arises.

I could tell a number of stories about hearing what our community needs and then responding, but here is the lesson I believe we have learned: if we are going to reach our community, then we have to know our community. The pastors and lay leaders in this book took the time to listen to single moms and superintendents, to drug addicts, and to children without proper nutrition. Then they responded. They made the decision not to be overwhelmed by the needs that exist in rural communities. Instead, they acted in faith and challenged their churches to think outside the box to see the church not just as a place to attend and worship but as a sending station to be equipped for ministry. That cultural shift does not happen naturally. Pastors have to lead the way.

## Leadership

Developing an outward focus entailed not only developing relevant ministries to attract community members but also identifying and training leadership for these ministries to ensure their continuation. The lay leaders of all three churches described the process for starting and leading ministries in their churches as collaborative, although the pastor was a vital part of the process. New Life–Barnett's lay leaders spoke of an open atmosphere in which the pastor encouraged and fostered ideas. They felt he would take their ideas seriously but trusted his judgement concerning whether to move forward with an idea or not. Lay leaders from both Licking Assembly and New Life–Farmington described an active, collaborative process in which the pastor ensures new ideas are aligned with the church's vision and culture, are fleshed out enough to be implemented, and then lets them "go with it."

New and revitalized ministries require increased involvement on the part of the congregation, including new lay leadership. Lay leaders from New Life–Barnett and New Life–Farmington noted the increased involvement of their congregations. Many members have gone from just being congregants to being actively involved in the church. Christopher from New Life–Farmington indicated 75 to 80 percent of the membership now engage in ministry. This increased involvement is the result of being asked by their pastors to lead or participate and seeing the positive effects new ministries are having on their churches. Christopher went on to suggest, these congregations see God working and want to be part of the action.

To ensure ministries continue, these pastors have also worked to increase the leadership base within their churches. According to Christopher Yoder, one of the lay leaders from New Life–Farmington, his pastor is constantly looking for ways to connect people with ministry. He also felt people wanted to be asked: "Unless you're asked, most people assume things are getting done." Pastor Kevin has created an expectation that leaders of ministries train and mentor people to take their place when the time is appropriate. The church expects ministries to develop ministry teams, with multiple people trained in the leadership role so that leadership is rotated among those volunteers to avoid burnout. In a similar vein, David Vernon, a lay leader from New Life–Barnett, stated he had gone "from leading ministries to leading people" to become leaders of those ministries.

Chapter 11 deals extensively with the leadership qualities of turnaround pastors and their effects on lay leaders. Here, suffice it to say that reversing the trend toward death demands strong pastoral leadership. Pastors cannot be lazy or hands-off leaders and expect change to happen. When people administer CPR to revive someone who is dying, they often break some of the person's ribs in the process. Reviving a dying church means taking drastic measures to get its heart beating again for the lost. And in that process, some people may be hurt along the way. Although bringing hurt to others is never the intention of any good shepherd, sometimes it results from the only action that can be taken.

## Hospitality

Although hospitality can be considered another aspect of culture, the idea emerged in the interviews so often it deserves separate consideration. All three pastors worked to improve, maintain, and expand the hospitality of their churches, in terms of both outward focus and the physical environment of the church. In addition to building relationships and involving more and more members in ministries, pastors looked to the physical plant of their churches to improve hospitality both among members and between members and visitors and newcomers.

One of Pastor JD's first observations was how quickly people cleared out of the building when the service ended: "By the time I walked from the pulpit to the front door, everyone's gone." He proposed the addition of a café, reconfiguring the space within the building to accommodate it. Although initial reactions to the idea were not overwhelmingly in favor, shortly after its addition, Pastor JD noticed "it now takes an hour to clear this building out after church because everybody is sticking around and visiting."

Pastor Paul described his older congregation's receptivity to new people as "lov[ing] new people with wide open arms" and being "naturally warm and open and loving." The lay leaders from Licking Assembly also expressed the friendliness and welcoming they experienced when they first attended during the initial stages of the turnaround. Josh Kane noted they were "very friendly" even though he was "a little different" (i.e., wearing shorts, sporting tattoos and gauged ears, dying his hair) and that "acceptance of that nature was cool." Pastor Paul's task, then, was to "build upon that friendliness." Unfortunately, the architectural shotgun style of their former building was not conducive to doing so. When the church needed more space to house its growing numbers, the natural inclination of this congregation to be welcoming influenced the architecture and appointments of their new building: wide-open designs, natural light, purposefully positioned furniture to facilitate group conversations, and a coffee bar that serves as a focal point for such interactions throughout the week for both members and the community.

Jason Finch came to New Life–Farmington during the early stages of its turnaround. He was "impressed with how personable and friendly the people were." He attributed their attitude to Pastor Kevin's commitment to building relationships within both the church and the community. New Life–Farmington also needed to update their facilities to reflect their hospitable character. Now, as people walk through the glass front doors, they enter a small but modern foyer, complete with a welcome kiosk. When Pastor Kevin commented on this renovation, he noted the foyer "is the first thing people see when they walk into the church, and I want them to see we care."

The facilities in these three churches now better reflect the warmth and friendliness of their congregations. Not only have relationships between members been strengthened through increased opportunities to gather and build community, but those visiting for the first time can also see the caring these congregations have for their churches, each other, and their communities. As Josh Kane said, it's a place to "build community," "to lean on each other," and to "love each other again."

Let me ease your fears, pastors. I am not suggesting you must spend thousands of dollars to remodel your lobby or open a café. I am suggesting you invest in your church with some paint, air freshener, and frequent cleaning (especially the restrooms and children's areas). Paint is not expensive, and the opportunity to get people involved in a work project can help build unity. A little bit of air freshener goes a long way. And a clean environment makes people feel the church cares about them. But aesthetic updates only scratch the surface of what it means to be hospitable. Ultimately, these aesthetic updates only make a place look better.

Pastors and church leaders, you absolutely must ask yourself an honest question: "Are we creating a warm and welcoming environment for everyone who comes through our doors?" I am blessed to have spoken at nearly four hundred churches around the world. I can honestly say most of them do not get hospitality right. Sure, someone stands at the door to hand people bulletins and possibly shake their hands. Some of these greeters are even friendly—if they know you. But newcomers are often left to wander around trying to find the restrooms. They don't know how to get to the sanctuary or whether a nursery is available. Church members just assume because they know what is happening and where everything is, then everyone else knows too. But they don't. Someone must help them!

The hospitality team was the first team I started after coming to Life Point Church. Even before we remodeled the lobby, we made sure that every person, regular attendee or visitor, felt they belonged. I am justifiably proud of the hospitality team at Life Point. Every time I talk with guests and they tell me, "I feel like everyone here loves me," my chest swells a bit (I think Jesus is happy about it too). I know we are not perfect in the area of hospitality, and sometimes someone gets missed (we're working on that). But when I look around and see newcomers engaged in conversation with church members and friends having conversation over coffee, I cannot help but be thankful. When I see newcomers return the next Sunday, I know—and so do the hospitality team members—it's because they truly believe they belong at Life Point.

# CHAPTER 9

# The Pattern within the Turnaround Experience

The information gathered from these three churches, their pastors, and their lay leaders reveals a consistent experiential pattern: birth, growth, decline, moments of stabilization, plateauing or further decline, the introduction of the turnaround pastor, crisis and change, and growth. The following figure illustrates this pattern.

**Pattern of turnaround experience.**

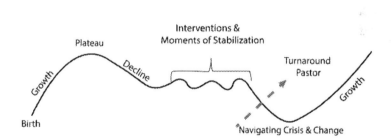

Figure 1

In previous decades, each of the three churches started with the dream of reaching their communities for Christ; and all experienced a time of extended growth. Pastors baptized converts and educated members in the ways of Christ. Congregations constructed buildings to accommodate their growth and formed ministries to serve their members and reach their rural communities. Pastors and congregations fervently served Christ and succeeded in building vibrant assemblies.

But various circumstances and challenges caused these same churches to falter. At New Life–Barnett, pastoral leadership issues brought problems causing a decline in attendance. At Licking Assembly, conflict between the pastor and deacons over the need to build a new building caused a church split. Soon after New Life Church–Farmington decided to build a new facility, conflict between the pastor and church arose resulting in a church split and a decline in attendance. Over time, each church plateaued and then declined in Sunday worship attendance, ministry effectiveness, and financial support. Although the reasons for the decline varied from church to church, the result was the same: an ineffective and dying local church body.

Attempts to reverse the downward trend included a multitude of pastoral transitions and interventions by denominational leadership. However, with the resignation or removal of each of the elected or appointed pastors, these churches lost momentum and returned to decline. This cycle of intervention, new pastors, moments of stabilization, and eventual decline was often repeated with little success.

With the appointment of the pastors highlighted in this book, the cycle of decline and death was broken. Working with key lay leaders, these turnaround pastors successfully navigated a myriad of crises, cultural changes, and leadership challenges to bring their churches back to health and growth. As shown in Table 3, these three churches managed tremendous turnarounds, as measured by Sunday worship attendance, over a span of five to eight years.

### Changes in Sunday Attendance at Participating Rural Assemblies of God Churches*

| Attendance | New Life-Barnett | Licking Assembly | New Life-Farmington |
|---|---|---|---|
| Highest prior to decline | 240 | 300 | 200 |
| At appointment of turnaround pastor | 30 | 30 | 40 |
| Current | 300 | 120 | 105 |
| Years | 5 | 8 | 6 |
| % Increase | 900 | 300 | 105 |

Table 3

* All attendance figures are self-reported by the churches.

Assemblies of God churches place a heavy emphasis on the local church pastor as the primary vision caster. Consequently, the pastor carries the sole responsibility for the decline or growth of a local church. When a church declines, the standard model of intervention is to recruit and appoint or elect another pastor. All three churches described here reported electing or having denominational leadership appoint multiple pastors during the declining years. Often, interim pastors filled the pulpit while the church considered the election of another pastor. Election of a new pastor often resulted in momentary stability and temporary growth; but sustained turmoil and declining membership eventually continued, leading each of these churches to come under the leadership of the Southern Missouri District Assemblies of God Council. Correspondingly, all three of the turnaround pastors considered here were appointed to their positions, not elected by their congregations.

What sets these pastors apart from those who could not affect the turnaround of these three churches? Pastors JD, Kevin, and Paul are similar in some respects but quite different in others.

At the time of their appointments to the senior pastorate, Pastor JD and Pastor Kevin were in their forties; Pastor Paul was in his twenties. All three pastors are married and some have children. None of the three pastors had experience as a senior pastor prior to being appointed to their present churches. Pastors JD and Paul had served as youth pastors in small rural churches. Pastor Kevin had served as associate pastor both at New Life–Farmington and at another church prior to the senior pastorate. Pastor Paul had also done pulpit supply work, filling in for pastors in small rural churches when needed.

In terms of training for their ministerial work, neither Pastor JD nor Pastor Paul had formal seminary training prior to their appointments. Pastor Paul attended college and, since coming to Licking Assembly, has attained two college degrees. He is working on his Master of Divinity degree. Prior to the turnaround years, New Life–Farmington had paid for the costs of Pastor Kevin's study materials to meet the requirements for ministerial credentials through the Assemblies of God.

All three pastors had grown up in or attended Assemblies of God churches. Pastor JD had also attended an urban inner-city church for a time. Pastor Paul had the unique experience as a child of having his father be his pastor when they attended a small nondenominational rural church. Pastor Kevin had joined New Life Church–Farmington as a teen and had spent most of his life there, apart from the few years he served as an associate pastor elsewhere.

Although all three pastors are now full-time senior pastors, Pastors JD and Paul first served their churches bi-vocationally. Pastor JD was a corporate executive prior to accepting the senior pastorate of New Life–Barnett and, because of the financial situation there, continued to work for that company for the first three years of his tenure at the church. Pastor Paul worked as the purchasing agent for a feedstore. Pastor Kevin did not have to take a job outside the church but came close to doing so when he realized the church could not afford to pay him. God's intervention through colleagues willing to subsidize his salary while the church got back on its feet financially averted the need to become a bi-vocational minister.

Perhaps the most important thing these three men had in common was not letting their lack of senior pastorate experience or extensive knowledge of turnaround principles and models hinder their mission. Instead, the lack of knowledge seemed to free these pastors to pursue paths of revitalization appropriate to their contexts. They did not know what to do, so they did what they knew to do and gathered people around them to make it happen. These pastors were leaders who assessed their current situations honestly and moved forward toward the goal of returning their churches to health and growth.

To reach their goal, all three pastors had to navigate crises and lead their churches through change. They used financial and cultural crises as platforms for building trust with their lay leaders and church members. Furthermore, these crises helped the pastors identify key lay leaders who helped them navigate changes needed immediately. With trust also came a willingness on the part of most congregants to help implement needed changes to revitalize their churches. Successfully navigating each crisis strengthened the bonds of trust between pastors, lay leaders, and church attendees as they collaborated to find solutions to their challenges. As trust continued to increase with their lay leaders, these pastors broadened the vision for their churches. They worked together to shift the attention of their congregations from an inside focus on organizational survival to an outward focus on engaging positively with their communities to influence people toward Christ.

Growth did not come to these churches because of a single event, program, or ministry. Every pastor gets hundreds of emails, advertisements, and snail mail touting the latest program that will "make your church grow." These promotions peddle quick answers to complicated problems that go deeper than a better ministry offering. Pastors, in their desire to see growth, "copy and paste" these programs without considering their effectiveness in a rural context. None of the pastors and lay leaders interviewed spoke about an "out of the box" program. Instead, they did the hard work of learning their communities. They spent time trying to understand the real needs and the real challenges their communities faced. Then they used that knowledge to develop ministries that made sense in their settings. These leaders' commitment to know their communities paid off in transformed lives.

None of the pastors or lay leaders interviewed could point to one single moment when they knew their churches would return to health and growth. When I asked each of them to describe that single "aha" moment when they just knew turnaround was happening, none of them could pinpoint that moment. Instead, they described a "fuzzy awareness" that their churches were beginning to turnaround. These pastors and lay leaders were so entrenched in the work of revitalization that their growth almost surprised them.

Ultimately, the turnaround of their churches resulted from a confluence of multiple moments. Lay leaders modeled a heart for service and sacrifice to the rest of the congregation. Pastors empowered lay leaders to do ministry by providing an environment in which new ideas were expected and encouraged. Pastors and lay leaders collaborated to bring ideas to reality, forming a vision for active ministry. As more attendees participated in ministry, these churches reached more people for Christ, and Sunday morning worship attendance increased.

# CHAPTER 10

# The Language of the Turnaround Experience

I n reading, writing, and reflecting on the information supplied by these pastors and lay leaders, I noticed several key words and phrases in their descriptions: *vision, willing, willingness, welcoming, friendly, friendliness, personable,* and *prayer.* This language reflects the powerful cultural change taking place in these turnaround churches. It is the language of people who have decided their churches should live and thrive.

Of these key words, *vision* appeared most frequently in the interview transcripts. Although one lay leader used the word to describe the supernatural experience of seeing something occur before it happened, the pastors and lay leaders primarily used vision to describe the picture of the future of their church. Vision is typically cast by the pastor and caught by the congregation, which carries it out in collaboration with the pastor. The vision is supported by church board members (or deacons), whose primary role is not financial or pastoral oversight but ensuring church core values are maintained. In catching the vision, congregants support and participate in ministries and church activities inspired by the vision.

For lay leaders, vision was the pastor's domain, which they then supported through their work. However, they also believed they were free to help their pastors shape the vision for their church. They felt their input and ideas about beginning or reforming ministries were vital to the pastors' vision and willingly submitted them for their critique and approval. In no small way, lay leaders and pastors engaged in open dialogue concerning the formation and implementation of ministries in support of the vision. One lay leader described his pastor as a "coach" who listens to ideas, helps form those ideas to fit the vision, and then empowers the leader to implement the idea.

**Willing and willingness.**

These words express the idea of vision and the heart or attitude of the congregation toward change. Catching the vision meant congregants were willing to support and participate in ministries and church activities inspired by the vision. Pastor JD described himself as being willing to tackle problems and challenges of all kinds "head on." His willingness, in turn, created trust in the people, who then became willing to make the deep sacrifices necessary to move the church forward. Another pastor declared, without people willing to work, his church could never have experienced turnaround. He used the word to describe that attitude of his church to take drastic steps to keep the church alive. This pastor also saw willingness as a valuable leadership characteristic and a determining factor for those asked to take on more significant leadership roles.

Willing and willingness also described the attitude toward change held by the lay leaders of these three churches. They recognized they must act if their churches were to survive. Doing nothing or resisting change for the sake of their comfort or position would not bring their churches back to health. Lay leaders were the "tip of the spear," modeling acceptance and enthusiasm for change to the larger church body. They worked hard to carry out their pastors' vision and to bring others on board. Their attitude of willingness created a ripple effect in their congregations, helping them become willing to see change in a positive light.

Lay leaders also used these two words to describe their churches' attitudes toward sacrifice. Those members who caught the vision cast by the pastor "stepped up" and gave their time, energy, and skills to help bring about change, even when the change brought emotional discomfort.

## Outside

The word *outside* appeared in the interviews multiple times. Pastors and lay leaders used this keyword in three different ways. One meaning of "outside" related to the missional activity of the church. One of the lay leaders referred to the church being "outside the church more than the inside," referring to the numerous ministry activities conducted to reach people for Christ in the area the church served. The intent of these activities, whether held at the physical church site or off campus, was to attract people who were not part of the church—in other words, those who were outside the local church body.

Participants also used "outside" in describing their cognitive understanding that the way in which members interact with community stakeholders is vital to the success of the church. How lay leaders and pastors manage their relationships with individuals who are not part of the church directly affects their communities' perceptions of the church. One pastor spoke of his awareness that his behavior in restaurants, retail stores, and other public places reflects on the church. As the Apostle Paul admonished believers at Colossae to "be wise in the way you act toward outsiders, making the most of every opportunity," pastors and lay leaders expressed a keen sense of responsibility to act wisely to those outside of their local assemblies.[74]

The third meaning of "outside" referred to people unconnected to the church pitching in to help with resources the church needed. One pastor spoke of individuals and businesses providing

---

74 Col 4:5 (NIV)

financial resources for the missional activity of the church even though they had no personal connection to the church. The pastors and lay leaders interviewed saw a correlative reality between a good reputation with outsiders and the outsiders' willingness to take part in church-sponsored activities. They saw the reputation of their churches in their communities as crucial for opening opportunities to serve their communities effectively and to influence people toward a relationship with Christ.

### Welcoming, friendly, friendliness, and personable

These four words constitute a word group because participants used them synonymously to describe an overarching concept of hospitality. Jason Finch correlated his pastor's personable character with the church's welcoming and friendliness to both attendees and guests. Two other lay leaders described their first experiences with their church as welcoming and friendly, despite the significant age difference between them and most of the congregants. Their pastor credited his church's friendly and welcoming culture as a vital characteristic of the church's growth. Although another pastor did not use these keywords specifically, he related his desire to create a physical environment in which church attendees and guests could get to know one another. To facilitate this vision, his church remodeled the expansive church foyer to accommodate a café.

Intentionality about creating a warm and welcoming environment served to build bridges between the church and its guests. Church attendees worked hard to involve themselves in the community through outreach events. The fruit of those hours was not only garnering influence in the community but also attracting guests to Sunday morning worship. The expectation was simple: the more people who come to Sunday worship, the greater the opportunity for people to receive Christ. Knowing that people from outside would be coming into their midst, the pastors of these three churches modeled hospitality for their congregations and encouraged them to show hospitality to all.

## Prayer

Prayer referred both to the source of inspiration for the churches' vision and to the appropriate reaction to church challenges. One lay leader directly attributed the decline of her church to its lack of corporate prayer. When the church began to pray together, "as a body, New Life–Barnett came alive." Prayer was the response to a need for volunteers to operate the growing number of ministries at the church as well. As one lay leader stated, "We need[ed] van drivers, so we prayed, and people stepped up!" Another lay leader pointed to prayer as the primary tool for resolving conflict among volunteers at his church. When a need arose to speak to a church attender concerning inappropriate behavior, the leaders of that church gathered to pray, get direction from the Lord, and then act on that direction.

Pastor Paul noted his decision-making process began with "being in my office before the Lord in prayer with a dream notebook." As he sought the Lord in prayer, God gave him direction for immediate challenges and vision for the future of the church. New Life–Farmington saw prayer as an opportunity to impact others for Christ. They called on their attendees to pray for a local police officer of their choosing for one year. These pastors and lay leaders saw prayer as a tool for influencing their local communities and creating opportunities for the involvement of those who, for various reasons, could not participate in events.

## Implications of the Turnaround Language

The common language reflected in the key words described above form a picture of the values found in rural Assemblies of God turnaround churches in Missouri. I suspect these values are present in other rural turnaround churches, despite their denominational affiliation. Vision is the domain of pastors. They cast vision, connect leaders to the various aspects of that vision, and coach those leaders to success. Vision is dependent on an attitude of willingness by church attendees and lay leaders to meet the challenges of turnaround and make necessary changes. Vision and a willingness to change set the stage for turning the church from an inside to an outside focus. An outside focus results in new and culturally-appropriate ministry formation, as well as the reforming of existing ministries necessary for the care of attendees and the growth of the church. As attendees interact with the outside community in meaningful ways, people from outside begin attending Sunday worship. Thus, the importance of a welcoming, friendly atmosphere becomes apparent.

Turnaround pastors emphasize the need for welcoming/friendliness by leading their churches to update or remodel facilities to create physical space for people to gather. Supporting these values is a belief that God is involved in the turnaround; therefore, pastors and lay leaders alike take their challenges and needs to God in prayer.

The language of turnaround is both descriptive and prescriptive. First, the language of turnaround describes the attitude necessary to bring about the revitalization of a declining church. Proverbs 29:18a (NIV) declares, "Where there is no revelation, people cast off restraint." Pastoral vision gives people courage to see beyond declining attendance and imagine a new and fruitful future. Clearly articulated vision challenges attendees to higher levels of commitment previously not demanded of them. The demands of the vision cause attendees to decide their level of willingness to participate in the ministries arising from the vision. Those attendees willing to work toward a better future are challenged to engage outsiders with the gospel, welcome the stranger into their midst, and express their dependency on God through prayer.

Second, the language of turnaround is prescriptive for church leaders considering revitalizing a church. Potential turnaround pastors need a vision for the future of the church. Their vision must include a call to the church body to reach those currently outside the Body of Christ, a plan for creating a hospitable church environment, and prayer. Pastors should call attendees to participate in the vision by creating avenues for open dialogue in which ideas relevant to reaching others are heard and considered. By articulating vision constantly and consistently, pastors create opportunities for church members to determine their level of personal participation. The more pastors cast vision, the better they can discern who is with them in fulfilling that vision. In doing so, potential turnaround pastors discover leaders among those participating and sharing in the vision to aid in the turnaround.

# CHAPTER 11

# The Realities of the Turnaround Experience

In the Introduction, I stated my aim is not to promote any one strategy or model that churches should employ to effect turnaround. Instead, my focus is to relay the lived experiences of the pastors and lay leaders in three rural Assemblies of God churches in Missouri that have gone from plateau and decline to health and vitality. Comparing their experiences to what is known about church revitalization in general, however, may prove enlightening.

### Church Plateau, Decline, and Turnaround

Although various church organizations define and measure church plateau and decline differently, most agree that a -2.5 percent change in worship attendance over a five- to ten-year period constitutes a decline. Conversely, a 2.5 percent increase in Sunday worship attendance over a five- to ten-year period constitutes a turnaround.[75] In addition to these quantitative measures, church organizations may use qualitative terms such as "losing momentum", "steep decline", or "survival" to describe declining churches.[76]

---

75 Clarensau, 2017; Costner, 2011; Martin, 2015; Penfold, 2011; Stetzer and Dodson, 2007.

76 Mays, 2011; Ross, 2013.

The three pastors interviewed here knew they were accepting pastorates of declining churches. The involvement of denominational leadership in their appointments was a clear indication these churches needed help. The lay leaders had observed dwindling attendance at Sunday worship and intuitively understood the need for strong leadership to revitalize their churches. They cited one of the main problems facing these new pastors as a lack of finances to meet obligations and do required maintenance. The general attitude permeating these churches was a lack of enthusiasm about the future of the church and their ability to sustain God's mission. Yet, despite the tremendous leadership, financial, spiritual, and cultural challenges, these lay leaders chose to stay to help find solutions.

The pastors and lay leaders I interviewed used both quantitative and qualitative measures to describe their turnaround experiences. The pastors knew the numeric size of their congregations at their appointment and could quickly relate their current size. As Assemblies of God pastors, they were accustomed to describing church metrics quantitatively through the Annual Church Ministry Report (ACMR). The denomination uses this tool to gather a wide range of data from its churches, including demographics, attendance, finances, programming, conversions, and baptisms. With this data, both the denomination and the individual churches get a quantitative snapshot of their growth or decline. The lay leaders, however, never showed the same awareness of exact attendance numbers. Instead, they spoke in ranges of numbers, instinctively knowing more people sat in the pews on Sunday and served in church ministries.

Pastors also know the power of story to help describe the growth or decline of the church. Although they report the quantitative data to their members each year, pastors are rooted in the lives of their church attendees and their communities. Telling stories of conversions, God's provision, and their church's participation in community events helps them accomplish ministry goals. The three pastors I interviewed served mostly blue-collar congregations who, as Pastor Paul Richardson explained, do not respond well to "MBA type presentations." They merely want to know that God has spoken to their pastors and then trust them to lead their churches forward.

The phenomenon of church turnaround can never solely revolve around quantitative percentages of decrease and increase. Creating a culture of change that leads to health and sustainability depends on the stories of changed hearts, changed attitudes, changed focus, and changed communities. Changing a deeply stagnant church culture requires pastors to lead their people into places where new stories can happen.

I served as a global missionary church planter to the Republic of South Africa for more than a decade. As I raised financial support for this mission, I stayed away from statistics and stuck to stories. My family and I spent three years volunteering in South Africa before I was appointed as a missionary. It was, quite honestly, the most exciting period of our lives as we lived on nothing by faith. During that three years, we helped to revitalize a church plant on the east side of Johannesburg, helped plant new churches, and taught at the Bible college in Pretoria. We came home with amazing stories of transformed lives.

Then, for eighteen months, my family and I crisscrossed the United States and Canada, telling those stories. People responded. They got it. They saw the little girl who showed up at church one morning, gave her life to Christ, and then proceeded to bring more than a dozen family members to Christ. They heard the powerful testimony of a grandmother on fire for Christ who held a children's prayer meeting in her home—a prayer meeting where verified miracles occurred on a regular basis. The power of these stories helped us raise our budget and get back to the field.

Pastor, does your church know its own story? Are you celebrating the wins—no matter how small? People in your congregation need to hear the stories of changed lives. They need to hear how their efforts are making a difference in the lives of real people in the community. Pastor, do you have some recent stories? Are you actively engaged in your community to the point where God can give you a story? I do not ask these questions to condemn or in any way cause guilt. I know the pressures of bi-vocational ministry in a small-town. But are you leading your church to a place where faith is required? A place where only God can get the glory? Or have you chosen to play it safe, circle the wagons, and keep people happy? Declining rural churches in the United States need a miracle to survive. They need leaders who have the faith to look at a valley of dry bones and, through the power of the Holy Spirit, call them to life.[77]

To identify the churches explored in this book, rural was defined as "all population[s], housing, and territory not included within an urbanized area or urban cluster."[78] Of the 114 counties in Missouri, 101 are classified as rural. Half of those have been declining in population, which leaves them with less political representation and fewer financial resources. As a result, communities in these areas often have limited access to needed social services to deal with problems such as alcohol and drug abuse and health care. According to the 2016 National Survey on Drug Use and Health, 37.8 percent of youths between the ages of twelve and twenty who live in nonmetropolitan areas use alcohol.[79] The report indicates 14.2 percent of children in nonmetropolitan areas use illicit drugs; 11.2 percent use marijuana. The Rural Matters Institute reports 16 percent of adults and 23 percent of children in rural communities live below the poverty level, and two thirds of rural communities have no access to mental health

---

77 See Ezek 37.
78 Ratcliffe et al., 2016, 3.
79 Substance Abuse and Mental Health Administration, 2017.

services.[80] The *2018 Missouri Poverty Report* indicates rural areas in Missouri also have limited access to healthcare.[81]

The three churches highlighted here created ministries to fill the social services and healthcare gaps in their communities. New Life–Barnett attacked the problem of alcoholism and drug addiction head on. Proverbs 7 Ministry initially began as a program dealing directly with substance abuse issues, but the lay leaders involved worked with their pastor to form ministries to help people with issues that often drive addiction, such as poor financial management. Leaders also urged adults participating in the recovery programs to bring their children to the Wednesday night meetings, leading to a burgeoning children's ministry where the children participate in age-appropriate activities and interact with church staff and volunteers. As a result of these ministries, which are a major part of the outreach of New Life–Barnett, lives are being changed and hearts transformed by the gospel.

Because these pastors and lay leaders believe the gospel can transform lives, they are involved in the messiness of the human condition. And, in doing so, they have brought about not only personal transformation but also church turnaround.

**Turnaround Pastors**

Rural churches require "intentional intervention and transformational change" to accomplish turnaround.[82] Transformational leaders are those who focus on achieving mutually shared goals above their self-interests. They are vision casters who influence followers to share in their vision through creativity and innovation. They also evidence several other transformational characteristics, many of which the three pastors and their lay leaders

---

80  Rural Matters Institute, 2017.
81  Missouri Community Action Network, 2018.
82  Russell, 2014, 36.

revealed during their interviews. Of those, six specific characteristics stood out:

- Leading by example
- Being transparent about church problems
- Establishing new expectations through vision
- Appealing to a higher cause
- Using crises to build trust
- Prioritizing relationship building

Identifying these pastoral characteristics serves two purposes.
First, denominational or church network leaders may use them
in forming a rubric for the assessment of pastoral candidates
considered for the leadership of declining churches. Second,
these characteristics may serve as a self-assessment evaluative
tool for pastors who are considering opportunities to lead dying
churches to health and growth.

## Leading by example

The turnaround of the participating churches required sacrifice on the part of all involved. The pastors modeled lives of sacrifice, inspiring their lay leaders and attendees to do the same.
These turnaround pastors were willing to pay a steep price for
change, as Stroh notes: "Turnaround is fairly rare, and that's
probably because it is often costly."[83] The act of accepting the
pastorate of a dying church is itself sacrificial:

- Pastor JD received no remuneration for his work for three
  years while driving over four hundred miles to the church
  each weekend.
- Pastor Paul received a salary from the church insufficient
  to provide adequate care for him and his wife.

---

83 Stroh, 2014, 138.

- Pastor Kevin recognized church finances were insufficient to pay him while trying to pay off debt accrued for a then unused building.

These pastors were also examples of faith. They believed their dying congregations could once again become thriving, vibrant parts of their communities. They had faith in their lay leaders, allowing them to form and re-form ministries to reach others for Christ. They challenged church attendees to try things previously untried in their churches:

- New Life–Barnett launched a successful recovery ministry to meet the challenges of alcoholism and drug addiction in its small community.
- Licking Assembly helped public school students learn basic life skills and ministered to single mothers in need of a helping hand.
- New Life–Farmington reached out to first responders in the county, offering spiritual care for them and their families.

These examples do not comprise an exhaustive list of new outreaches. Instead, they demonstrate how the faith of a pastor in the people in the congregation can inspire different ways of reaching new people for Christ.

## Being transparent about church problems

Repeatedly, the pastors interviewed stood before their congregations to explain a host of challenges to the sustainability of their churches, including challenges with banks, unpaid bills, and ineffective ministries. These pastors withstood the emotional pain of taking on problems they had no hand in creating and never laid the blame for these challenges at the feet of previous pastors or the lay leaders. Instead, they owned the problems, spoke honestly about the issues, and refused to be defeated.

More important, these pastors always asked their lay leaders and church attendees to take ownership of the problems and help find solutions. Taking ownership led individual church attendees to be generous, offering to pay overdue bills, to give their time and talents to do specific projects to save money, and to become involved in ministry endeavors. In being transparent about church problems, these pastors helped their church attendees and lay leaders to grasp how much help the church required to stay viable and to respond positively.

### Establishing new expectations through vision

Upon accepting their appointments, the pastors herein inherited multiple problems. Church buildings were often in disrepair, in need of long-overdue maintenance. New Life–Farmington was on the brink of losing its building because of declining attendance and finances. New Life–Barnett had overbuilt during good years. Now, in decline, the building had become a financial drain on the small congregation. Chaotic behavior during church services disguised as spirituality turned newcomers away. A belief that planning was unspiritual and hindered God's ability to work in the church permeated the culture of New Life–Barnett. Overall, financial problems, the moral failures of previous pastors, and a general belief that rural churches cannot attract quality pastors created low expectations in all three churches.

As each pastor clearly articulated his vision for his church, new expectations emerged. Vision became the foundation for church culture and the strategy for reaching others for Christ. Because all three pastors believed the vision for their churches was God-given and biblically accurate, they also believed God would provide the resources necessary to accomplish that vision.

Turnaround pastors acted in faith and challenged lay leaders and church attendees to do the same.

Vision cast by these pastors led to new expectations for attendees. These, in turn, led to the churches taking purposeful action and their attendees becoming meaningfully involved in their communities. The focus of ministry was no longer exclusively on the existing membership. Instead, each church actively entered its community and intentionally sought out ways to help. The new expectation of new people from the community attending Sunday worship led to the renovation of deteriorating church facilities to create warm, welcoming, caring environments. Repairing and updating facilities also reflected the expectation of good stewardship. Because of new expectations about financial management, church attendees felt more secure about the future of their churches; and communities knew these churches would honor their obligations.

New expectations also meant challenges from some attendees who did not believe in the need for change. These pastors confronted those who caused dissension or division in a loving but resolute manner. The visions for a healthy and vibrant church would not be derailed by those who refused to change. Confrontations were corrective, not punitive, allowing attendees involved the opportunity for reflection. As a result, all three pastors proudly proclaimed that most of the people who were members when they accepted their appointments remained members of their churches.

Rural church turnaround is the hardest assignment I have tackled in my nearly thirty years of ministry. Unlike the three pastors interviewed here, I cannot boast that most of the people attending the church when I came have remained. It took a while for me to come to grips with what I felt was a gross leadership misstep. No one, especially pastors, want to feel like they have disappointed people. No one likes the feeling of rejection that comes when church members leave to attend another church. I once described that feeling as akin to being slapped repeatedly in the face while being told "I love you." It hurts! It is confusing! But you persevere and you refuse to become bitter.

The reality of the challenges and the potential for hurt, confusion, and burnout in working to reverse the decline of churches is why turnaround pastors need grit. According to Angela Duckworth and colleagues, grit is "perseverance and passion for long-term goals"[84] and is the "one personal quality shared by prominent leaders in all fields."[85] Any pastor choosing to lead a rural church to revitalization must have this quality. Edward Hallowell, in his book *Shine: Using Brain Science to Get the Best from Your People*, insists no one knows where grit comes from but assumes it is a product of one's environment.[86]

What does grit look like in a turnaround pastor? In developing a profile of a turnaround pastor, Dr. Gordon Penfold found pastors with grit described themselves as focused, determined, outgoing, energetic, and innovative team builders who excel in communication and delegation.[87] They navigate personality clashes and negative attitudes toward change almost daily. Nevertheless, they tenaciously hold onto the vision God has put in their hearts for the church. In other words, the evidence of grit in turnaround pastors is their tenacity in clinging to God-given vision despite obstacles and conflict.

### Appealing to a higher cause

Change for the sake of change is an enemy of leadership. Change must connect to a reason if people are to support it. The turnaround pastors considered here were adept at connecting the changes they knew must occur to a higher cause:

---

84  Duckworth et al., 2007, 1087.
85  Duckworth et al., 2007, 1087.
86  Hallowell, 2011, 150.
87  Penfold, 2011, 162.

- Changing from an inward to an outward focus appealed to bringing the lost to Christ. The pastors challenged their churches to think about the awesomeness of people "getting saved" (a colloquialism for someone coming into relationship with Christ) at their altars.
- Launching children's and youth ministries appealed to the hope of these elderly and aging congregations for future generations to carry on the work of the church.
- Giving generously to global and local missions appealed to connecting these churches and their members to their local communities and beyond.
- Connecting the need for change to God's integrity, the good name of the church, and the glory of God helped congregants see a bigger picture of the work of God in their communities.

In appealing to a higher cause, these pastors ultimately explained the why undergirding the requested changes. They also tamped down the ideas that they were seeking change for the sake of change and that they were trying to make these churches do things the churches didn't want to do. Connecting change with a higher cause also gave these churches a sense of legacy as change became the opportunity for their churches to serve future generations.

## Using crises to build trust

The three pastors faced major crises early in their appointments to these declining churches. The timing of these crises seemed providential, giving these pastors opportunities to build trust with their attendees and lay leaders. Attendees often felt hopeless to change their situation as people left, financial contributions decreased, ministry programs faltered, and worship lacked energy and vibrancy. These turnaround pastors met enormous challenges to the viability of their churches head on, demonstrating strong leadership. They did not walk away from the challenges these situations brought. Instead, they committed to staying and walking with the people in their churches as they worked through difficult, potentially catastrophic, problems. They acted in faith and trusted in God as they confronted issues directly and engaged in firm decision-making. Through their actions, these pastors showed attendees they could lead their churches to sustainability.

Even so, dealing with crisis after crisis is mind numbing. I remember walking into the church, falling at the altar, and begging God to release me from leading Life Point Church. For the first two years, I dreaded every Monday morning because I knew it would bring one more disappointment. Someone would call to complain about the sermon. Others would call to rebuke my handling of some situation. Still others would drop by the office to "have a chat," which is code for "you stink as a pastor and I want to remind you of that fact." But amid all the financial, leadership, social, and other real pressures, God was working to shape my leadership as a turnaround pastor.

Somewhere I picked up this adage, which I have found to be true: Don't waste a crisis.[88] Every time we deal with a crisis, get input from others, and find solutions, our credibility rises. Credibility is the foundation for effectively leading change—and no one increases credibility through good preaching. Credibility comes as people watch us take on the hardest of challenges with faith, courage, and an undying belief that God and His people will find the right solution.

**Prioritizing relationship-building**

---

88  See Himelfarbe, 2010. The most recent variation of this statement is attributed to Rahm Emanuel, White House Chief of Staff to President Barak Obama; however, its use can be traced to Niccolo Machiavelli.

The priority these three pastors placed on relationship-building emerged in a variety of ways. First, they went to great lengths to create physical spaces in their church buildings to accommodate human interaction. Because of growth, Licking Assembly moved from a small church building in which the foyer acted like a "cattle chute" to one with an expansive foyer designed for people to "hang out" and drink coffee.[89] New Life–Barnett tore out walls to expand its foyer to make space for a café, which has become a place people meet after church to share in each other's lives. Pastor JD believed the distance between people in rural communities causes isolation and that the church can play a vital role in relieving that isolation by bringing people together. Physical space, however, was only one part of the relationship priority.

When I interviewed them, none of these turnaround pastors depended on formal gifts assessments to determine ministry placement. Instead, they identified potential leaders through relationships, relying on knowing their people and then asking them to serve in places they believed were good for them. Relationships developed as pastors, lay leaders, and attendees worked on a variety of projects together or conversed while driving together. These opportunities allowed pastors to recognize attendees' gifts and areas of interest. As needs for ministry volunteers and leaders arose, the pastors connected attendees based on their gifting and interests rather than simply filling vacancies. In turn, the pastors asked their lay leaders to build strong relationships with their ministry teams.

One of the assumptions undergirding my exploration of revitalizing rural churches was that turnaround pastors are transformational leaders. Bernard Bass asserts, "among Methodist

---

89  A cattle chute uses metal fencing to create a narrow opening for cattle moving from one area to another or onto a vehicle. The chute only for allows cattle to move in a single-line formation, letting the farmer efficiently control, count, and vaccinate animals as they move through the opening.

ministers, transformational – not transactional – leadership was positively related to high church attendance among congregants and growth in church membership."[90] Transformational leaders focus on achieving mutually shared goals above their own self-interests by casting vision with clarity and influencing followers to share in that vision by promoting follower creativity and innovation. My interviews with all the pastors and lay leaders confirmed my assumption. The three pastors demonstrated the four key components of a transformational leadership style: idealized influence, inspirational motivation, intellectual stimulation, and individualized concern.[91]

*Idealized Influence* and *Inspirational Motivation* is about vision, motivation, and modeling behavior for followers to emulate. Transformational leaders clearly articulate vision portraying an optimistic future. They motivate by showing followers how they can contribute to, enhance, and share in the vision they are casting. Then, the transformational leader models the vision he or she has presented to followers "by behaving in admiral ways that cause followers to identify with the leader."[92] *Intellectual Stimulation* occurs when "the leader helps followers to become more innovative and creative."[93] *Individualized Consideration* occurs as the leader gives his or her time to followers as a coach and mentor to assist them in their growth and development. Ultimately, transformational leaders emphasize the values of followers above their self-interests.[94]

By clearly articulating a God-given vision, the turnaround pastors presented in this book portrayed hopeful and optimistic futures for their churches. They motivated followers by connecting their gifts and interests to the vision in meaningful ways,

---

90  Bass, 1990, 22
91  Bass and Riggio, 2006.
92  Judge and Piccolo, 2004, 755.
93  Bass, 1999, 11
94  Jandaghi et al., 2009

allowing followers to see how they were positively contributing to the fulfillment of the vision. These pastors led their followers by being exemplars of the vision they were casting. They made room for individual followers to use their creativity to develop new ministries to reach others for Christ. They paid attention to individuals offering suggestions and plans for new endeavors and solutions. Then, acting as coaches, these turnaround pastors helped their followers successfully design and implement ministries and programs in their churches and communities.

Let's face it, pastors are in the people business. Yet this is a part of ministry I have struggled with since my call. I am an introvert. There, I said it. I am not the life of the party. I am more the type who likes to stand in the corner, munch on a few hors d'oeuvres, and avoid small talk. Early in my ministry career, a Bible college professor informed us that introverts were not made for the pastorate. Instead, the pastorate was reserved for extroverts who could light up a room and make lots of friends. Taking the word of this professor, I spent the next twenty-five years trying to overcome my broken personality. The result was twofold. First, I was a fake and everyone knew it. Second, I was frustrated with trying to be something I am not. But we are in the people business and introverts are not about people, right? Wrong.

My life was changed by Susan Cain's book, *Quiet: The Power of Introverts in a World That Can't Stop Talking*.[95] This magnificent book taught me that I was not broken because of my introversion. I learned I could effectively build relationships, just in a different way. I stopped being frustrated with my lack of ability to make small talk and relished in my ability to focus intently on the person in front of me without being distracted by everything else going on around me. In the last few years, I have embraced my quietness and channeled that energy into building

---

95  Cain, 2012.

deep relationships with my wife, kids, and many of the people in my church.

The most valuable commodity in the rural context is not money or buildings; it's relationships. So, if you want to bring about change effectively, you must be intentional about building and maintaining relationships with church members and community stakeholders, regardless of your personality bent. Embrace who you are and use your strengths to build strong personal relationships.

## Lay Leaders

According to current research, transformational leaders consistently produce four follower effects: admiration, loyalty, trust, and respect.[96] Followers of transformational leaders also often experience changes in their attitudes[97] and increase their commitment to change.[98] As their trust in these leaders grows, so does their achievement.[99] The lay leaders interviewed herein clearly articulated four positive effects the three turnaround pastors had on them:

- Lay leaders felt empowered to minister.
- Lay leaders trusted their pastors to coach them to success.
- Lay leaders sacrificed their time and energy because they believed in their pastor's vision.
- Lay leaders developed a deep trust in their pastor.

These lay leaders overwhelming believed they were free to create ministry and carry it out. Few things make someone feel more vulnerable than presenting an idea to a superior. Because

---

96  Bass and Avolio, 1994.
97  Conger et al., 2000.
98  Michaelis et al., 2010.
99  Conger et al., 2000; Podsakof et al., 1990.

Assemblies of God churches lean toward a culture in which the pastor is the primary visionary, church members are often reticent to offer new ideas for fear of rejection. Or, because the pastor is viewed as the primary creator of ideas, not church members or leaders. That was not the case with these three churches. These lay leaders brought ideas to their pastors and fully expected those ideas to be validated. However, they also submitted those ideas to the authority of their pastors and to their pastors' perceptions of how their ideas fit into the broader vision of the church.

The lay leaders also believed their pastors would coach them to success. After listening to their ideas, the pastors helped their lay leaders form those ideas to fit the vision and then empowered them to implement the ideas. Shaping the ideas often took place through dialogue, allowing these people to feel they could dream about the future of their church along with their pastor. This sense of belonging gave them ownership of the church's vision, which further empowered them to seek God, notice ministry opportunities in their communities, and believe their contributions to the vision mattered.

As lay leaders caught the pastoral vision in their church, they took it heart and were willing to go above and beyond to make that vision happen. These lay leaders followed the example of their pastors and worked alongside their pastors to plan and execute outreach events in their communities. They gave inordinate amounts of volunteer time to their churches, with some spending more than seventy hours per week on remodeling projects. Others sacrificed two to three evenings every week to serve children and adults involved in church ministries. Although the value of the time they invested and the money they saved their churches is hard to measure, their sacrifices were vital to the turnaround of these churches.

Over time and through experience, lay leaders began to believe their pastors would do what was right for their church.

They quickly adopted their pastor's vision of change. Working in partnership with their pastor, managing crises, implementing change, and celebrating even the smallest victories created a powerful bond of trust. This trust then spilled over into the lives of other attendees.

Costner defines a high-capacity lay leader as someone who, "[understands] their God-given purpose and calling, [has] a mindset of growth, [possesses a] servant's heart, and desire[s] to multiply and grow the body of Christ."[100] The individuals highlighted here were clearly high-capacity lay leaders. They believed their contributions played a vital role in their churches returning to health. They felt their turnaround pastors were not only spiritual leaders but also friends. They showed due respect and deference to their pastor as leader but felt they were part of a team that was making an impact on their communities. None of these lay leaders were employees of their church. They volunteered their time because they wanted their churches to grow and the Gospel to be spread around the world.

---

100 Costner, 2017, 133–34.

# CHAPTER 12

# Revitalizing Small Rural Churches

The need for turnaround pastors is evident in the continuing decline of rural churches, many of which are teetering on the brink of closing. However, even the most capable pastors cannot successfully carry out God's mission without the help of capable and willing lay leaders. In turn, pastors need to help their lay leaders become as effective as possible. To build leadership within the congregation and to effect turnaround, pastors must be transformational in their leadership practice.

The three pastors and ten lay leaders who allowed me to probe their experiences tell a compelling story of God's grace and desire to see dead churches in forgotten places live again. In viewing these three turnaround churches through an ecclesiastical lens, we see that these pastors exemplify the functional roles and biblical qualities of pastors found in the New Testament:

- They are preachers and teachers, involved in the betterment of their congregants and communities.
- They are shepherds, guiding the spiritual direction of their churches.
- They are elders and bishops, overseeing the administrative needs of their congregations.

As such, these three turnaround pastors are fulfilling the goal identified in Ephesians 4:12 (NIV) by: "prepar[ing] God's people for works of service, so that the body of Christ may be built up."

The demographic and geographic realities of rural communities validate the need for churches to insert themselves into the social needs of their communities. The three turnaround pastors considered here positively confront the social issues in their communities, challenging their congregations to engage with people outside of Sunday worship. The poverty associated with many rural communities limits families' abilities to enjoy social activities. These three churches either create social events for their communities or partner with other organizations to do so. These events provide a safe place for children and families to participate at little to no cost and create avenues for church members to serve their neighbors. Lay leaders within these churches also recognize issues negatively impacting their communities (e.g., drug and alcohol addiction, financial problems, single parenting) and, empowered by their pastors, create ministries to reach those people affected. In turn, as these churches shift their focus and reach out to their communities, people from outside the church start coming to Sunday worship and joining these congregations.

The priorities of rural and nonrural churches are the same in terms of content but different in terms of rank order. However, for turnaround pastors, the first priority is cultivating relationships. As transformational leaders, the three pastors I interviewed exemplify this focus on relationships. Using relational approaches, they advance their vision for the church, identify and develop leadership, and build bridges between the mission of the church and the communities they serve. Through strong relationships with church leaders and stakeholders, these pastors implement change initiatives, manage crises, and create opportunities for involvement in their communities.

Successful turnaround pastors cast a clear vision for prayer, outreach, and hospitality. Because a well-articulated vision draws attendees to participate in the vision, turnaround pastors invite attendees to share in the vision through input and participation. Eventually, some of these participants become key lay leaders. Pastors JD, Paul, and Kevin clearly evidence the qualities of transformational leaders as they work with their congregations to revitalize their churches. They lead by example, are transparent about church problems, establish new expectations through vision, appeal to a higher cause to effect change, and build trusting relationships with their followers.

Because small churches rely heavily on members instead of paid staff to lead ministries and perform administrative functions, growing and developing these lay leaders is vital. The lay leaders from New Life–Barnett, Licking Assembly, and New Life–Farmington actively participate in their pastor's vision, feeling empowered to minister, trusting their pastor to coach them to success, and giving sacrificially of their time and energy to bring the pastor's vision to reality.

How pastors and lay leaders effect turnaround will be unique to the contexts of their churches and the communities they serve. None of the turnaround pastors highlighted here attended revitalization seminars, workshops, or conferences. They had no experience as lead pastors and knew little, if anything, about church revitalization methods or models. Instead, they were adept and intentional about building relationships. When transformational leaders are present, declining churches can navigate successfully to health and vitality.

As a rural turnaround pastor, I am personally aware of the challenges presented to leaders who endeavor to move a church body forward from death to life. Congregations experiencing decline tend to do so because they have shifted from an evangelistic mindset to one of maintenance or survival. Moving a congregation toward an outwardly focused paradigm is difficult and presents many opportunities for both pain and joy. Pain in watching people leave the congregation due to misunderstanding. Pain in listening to accusations of authoritarianism, disrespect, compromise, and even heresy. Pain in managing division in the church body and a general disdain for those outside the Body of Christ. As I stated earlier, revitalizing a rural church has been the hardest ministry assignment of my life.

But it is also one of the most rewarding. There is joy as something dead comes alive again. Joy as new leaders emerge and old leaders catch the new vision. Joy as unity overtakes division and God's people get a fresh vision to reach those far from God. Joy as new believers begin to serve the local church. Joy in the smallest of victories. And, yes, over time and through prayer, joy in even the most frustrating parts of this whole journey.

My prayer for you is that, in all the "stuff" involved in rural church turnaround, you "let the peace of Christ rule in your hearts."[101]

---

101 Col 3:15 (NIV)

# Bibliography

Bass, Bernard M. "From Transactional to Transformational Leadership: Learning to Share the Vision." *Organizational Dynamics* 18 no. 3 (1990) 19–31. http://cupdx.idm.oclc. org login?url=http://go.galegroup.com.cupdx.idm oclc. org/ps/i.do?p=AONE&sw=w&u.conu &v=2.1&it=r&id= GALE%7CA8201994&asid=239df573dfbab884cc348de2 e1d17a5c

———. *Leadership and Performance beyond Expectations.* New York: Free, 1985.

———. "Two Decades of Research and Development in Transformational Leadership." *European Journal of Work and Organizational Psychology* 8 no. 1 (1999) 9–32.

Bass, Bernard M., and Bruce J. Avolio. *Improving Organizational Effectiveness through Transformational Leadership.* Thousand Oaks, CA: Sage, 1994.

Bass, Bernard M., and Ronald E. Riggio. *Transformational Leadership.* 2nd ed. Mahwah, NJ: Lawrence Earlbaum, 2006.

Bossidy, Larry, and Ram Charan. Execution: *The Discipline of Getting Things Done.* New York: Crown Business, 2002.

Bridges, William. *Managing Transitions: Making the Most of Change.* 4th ed. Boston: DaCapo Lifelong Books, 2017.

Burns, James MacGregor. Leadership. New York: Harper & Row, 1978.

Cain, Susan. *Quiet: The Power of Introverts in a World That Can't Stop Talking.* New York: Crown, 2012.

Carney, Joseph. "Pastoral Leadership in a Rural Congregation." DMin diss. Winebrenner Theological Seminary, 2010.

ProQuest Dissertations. http://search.proquest.com / docview/856900848/

Clarensau, M. "Growing, Plateaued, and Declining Churches." *2017 Assemblies of God Church Growth Report*, 2017. Available by request from Assembly of God office of statistics.

Conger, Jay A., et al. "Charismatic Leadership and Follower Effects." *Journal of Organizational Behavior* 21 no. 7 (2000) 747–67. Retrieved from http://www.jstor.org. cupdx.idm.oclc .org/stable/3100311

Costner, Matthew J. "Defining Characteristics of Laity among Turnaround Churches in the Carolinas." DMin diss. Biola University, 2017. ProQuest Dissertations. http://search .proquest.com/docview/1890207473/

Covey, Sean. *The 4 Disciplines of Execution*. New York: Free, 2012.

Crandall, Ron. *Turnaround Strategies for the Small Church*. Edited by Herb Miller. Nashville, TN: Abingdon, 1995.

Cromartie, John. "How Is Rural America Changing." *America by the Numbers*. Economic Research Service, United States Department of Agriculture. C-SPAN broadcast, May 24, 2013. https://www.census.gov/newsroom/cspan/rural_ america/20130524_rural_america _slides.pdf

Cromartie, John, and Shawn Bucholtz, S. "Defining the 'Rural' in Rural America." *Amber Waves of Grain* (June 1, 2008). https://www.ers.usda.gov/amber-waves/2008/june / defining-the-rural-in-rural-america/

Cunningham, Christine L. "Critically Reflective Leadership." *Australian Journal of Teacher Education 37* no. 4 (2012) 46–58. http://ro.ecu.edu.au/cgi/viewcontent. cgi?article=1744 &context=ajte

Daman, Glen C. "Why the Rural Church Matters." *Facts and Trends* (May 18, 2018). https://factsandtrends. net/2018/05/18/why-the-rural-church-matters.

Davis, Danny Wade. "The Lived Experiences of Pastors and Lay Leaders in Turnaround Rural Assembly of God Churches in Missouri: A Hermeneutic and Phenomenological Study." EdD diss. Concordia University-Portland, 2019. https://commons.cu-portland.edu edudissertation/245

Duckworth, Angela, et al. "Grit: Perseverance and Passion for Long-Term Goals." *Journal of Personality and Social Psychology* 92 no. 6 (2007) 1087–101.

Dudley, Carl, and David A. Roozen. *Faith Communities Today: A Report on Religion in the United States Today.* Hartford, CT: Hartford Institute for Religion Research, 2001.

Farley, Gary, et al. *The Rechurching of Rural America: A Report of the Restudy of Rural Churches in America.* 2005. https://www.ruralchurch.us/rechurching

Frazee, Randy. *The Comeback Congregation: New Life for a Troubled Ministry.* Edited by Lyle E. Schaller. Nashville, TN: Abingdon, 1995.

Fullan, Michael. *Change Leader: Learning to Do What Matters Most.* San Francisco: Jossey-Bass, 2011.

Hallowell, Edward M. *Shine: Using Brain Science to Get the Best from Your People.* Boston: Harvard Business, 2011.

Harris, Joe, et al. "USDA Rural in Character Guidance." *Washington Report* (October 30, 2017). https://www.nar.realtor/washington-report/usda-rural-in-character-guidance

Hartford Institute for Religion Research. *Fast Facts about American Religion.* Hartford, CT: Hartford Seminary, Hartford Institute for Religion Research, n.d. http://hirr.hartsem.edu /research/fastfacts/fast_facts.html

Herrold, Benjamin. "Numerous Factors Drive Missouri's Rural Population Trends." *AgUpdate* (June 10, 2017). https://www.agupdate.com/news/rural_life/numerous-factors-drive-missouri-s-rural-population-trends/article_2f355b96-ae04-5d16-9834-24b832f6280e.html

Himelfarb, Alex. "Never Waste a Good Crisis." *Alex's Blog.* (May 14, 2010). http://afhimelfarb .wordpress. com/2010/05/14/never-waste-a-good-crisis

Hoskins, Rob. "What You Don't Know about Rural America: 3 Common. Misconceptions." *Rural Matters Institute* (September 26, 2017). https://www.bgcruralmatters. com/what-you-dont-know-about-rural-america-3-common-misconceptions/

Hughes, Tawney A. "Idealized, Inspirational, and Intellectual Leaders in the Social Sector: Transformational Leadership and the Kravis Prize." Thesis. Claremont McKenna College, 2014. CMC Senior Theses, 906. http;//scholarship.claremont.edu/cmctheses/906

Hunt, Terry. "Shifting a Small Rural Congregation's Understanding of Church Leadership." DMin diss. Garrett-Evangelical Theological Seminary, 2016. ProQuest Dissertations (10127138). http://search.proquest.com/docview/1809746545/

Jandagh, Gh., et al. "Comparing Transformational Leadership in Successful and Unsuccessful Companies." *International Journal of Economics and Management Engineering* 2 no. 5 (2008) 621–6. https://waset.org/publications/5570/comparing-transformational-leadership-in-successful-and-unsuccessful-companies

Johnson, Kenneth. *Demographic Trends in Rural and Small-Town America.* Durham, NH: Carsey Institute, 2006.

———. "Where Is 'Rural America,' and What Does It Look Like?" *The Conversation* (February 20, 2017). http://theconversation.com/where-is-rural-america-and-what-does-it-look-like-72045

Judge, Timothy A., and Ronald F. Piccolo. "Transformational and Transactional Leadership: A Meta-Analytic Test of Their Relative Validity. *Journal of Applied Psychology* 89 no. 5 (2004) 755–68.

Kandle, William, and John Cromartie. "New Patterns of Hispanic Settlement in Rural America." Rural Development Research Report RDRR-99. United States Department of Agriculture, Economic Research Service, 2004. https://pdfs.semanticscholar.org/8afa /903dd4e32e-0103b11bcea0955ba8af980332.pdf

Kouzes, James M., and Barry Z. Posner. *The Leadership Challenge: How to Make Extraordinary Things Happen in Organizations*. San Francisco: Jossey-Bass, 2017.

Lamb, Marcell Allen. "Exploration into Small, Rural, Declining, Near End of Life-Cycle Church Turnaround in the Wesleyan and United Methodist Church." DMin diss. Asbury Theological Seminary, 2016. ProQuest Dissertations. http://search.proquest.com/docview /1796968926/

Martin, J. Bradley. "Church Turnaround: A Study of Formerly Declining Churches That Are Growing." DMin diss. Asbury Theological Seminary, 2015. ProQuest Dissertations. http://search.proquest.com/docview/1752405880/

Maybue, R. "Rediscovering Pastoral Ministry." *In Pastoral Ministry: How to Shepherd Biblically*, by John F. MacArthur and the Master's Seminary Faculty, 3–14. Nashville, TN: Thomas Nelson, 2005.

Mays, Ronald Brent. "Comparing Turnaround Leadership in a Rural Church and in Schools." 2011. PhD diss. University of Louisville, 2011.ProQuest Dissertations (3479934) http://search.proquest.com/docview/896956701/

McEachin, Helen J. "Assessing the Perception and Practice of Servant Leadership in Small Rural Protestant African-American Churches." EdD diss. University of Phoenix, 2011. ProQuest Dissertations (3480372). http://search.proquest.com/docview /900302520/

McIntosh, Gary. *One Size Doesn't Fit All: Bringing Out the Best in Any Size Church*. Grand Rapids, MI: Fleming H. Revell, 1999.

Metaxes, Eric, and Stan Guthrie. "Reviving the Churches of Rural America: One Sheep at a Time." *Breakpoint* (blog), October 6, 2017. http://www.breakpoint.org/2017/10 / breakpoint-reviving-the-churches-of-rural-america/

Michaelis, Bjorn, et al. (2010). "Shedding Light on Followers' Innovation Implementation Behavior." *Journal of Managerial Psychology* 25 no. 4 (2010) 408–29.

Missouri Community Action Network. *2018 Missouri Poverty Report*. Jefferson City, MO: Missourians to End Poverty, 2018. http://www.caastlc.org/wpsite/ wp-content/uploads/2018/03/MCAN-MEP-2018- MissouriPovertyReport-DigitalDownload.pdf

National Congregations Study. *Religious Congregations in 21st Century America*. Durham, NC: National Congregations Study, 2012. http://www.soc.duke.edu/natcong/Docs/ NCSIII _report_final_tables.pdf

Nixon, David F. *Leading the Comeback Church: Help Your Church Rebound from Decline*. Kansas City: Beacon Hill, 2004.

Ogne, Steve, and Tim Roehl. *Tranformissional Coaching: Empowering Leaders in a Changing Ministry World*. Nashville, TN: B&H, 2008.

Penfold, Gordon Everett. "Defining Characteristics of Turnaround Pastors among Evangelical Churches in the Rocky Mountain States" DMin thesis. Biola University, 2011. ProQuest Dissertations & Theses Global (3455249). http://cupdx.idm.oclc.org /login?url=http://search. proquest.com.cupdx.idm.oclc.org/docview/868573448 ?accountid=10248

Penn, Phebian. "Charismatic and Transformational Leadership of Leaders in a Small African American Church."

EdD diss. University of Phoenix, 2011. ProQuest Dissertations (3463508). http://search.proquest.com/docview/879421580/

Podsakof, Phillip M., et al. "Transformational Leader Behaviors and Their Effects on Followers' Trust in Leader, Satisfaction, and Organizational Citizenship." *Leadership Quarterly* 1 no. 2 (1990) 107–42.

Rainer, Thom S. "Dispelling the 80 Percent Myth of Declining Churches." Thom S. Rainer *Growing Churches Together,* June 28, 2017. http://thomrainer.com/2017/06/dispelling-80-percent-myth-declining-churches/

———. *Surprising Insights from the Unchurched and Proven Ways to Reach Them.* Nashville, TN: Zondervan, 2001.

Rainer, Thom S., and Charles E. Lawless. *Eating the Elephant: Leading the Established Church to Growth.* Crestwood, KY: Pinnacle, 2003.

Ratcliffe, Michael, et al. "Defining Rural at the U.S. Census Bureau." Report No. ACSGEO–1, American Community Survey and Geography Brief, United States Census Bureau, December 8, 2016. https://www2.census.gov/geo/pdfs/reference/ua/Defining_Rural.pdf

Robinson, Ken. *Out of Our Minds: Learning to Be Creative.* 2nd ed. West Sussex, UK: Capstone, 2011.

Ross, Donald. *Turnaround Pastor: Pathways to Save, Revive and Build Your Church.* Montlake Terrace, WA: Turnaround Church Coaching Network, 2013.

Rowold, Jens. "Effects of Transactional and Transformational Leadership of Pastors." *Pastoral Psychology* 56 no. 4 (2008) 403–11.

Rural Matters Institute. "Rural Matters: Planting, Revitalizing, Resourcing and Sustaining Life-Giving, Spirit-Filled Ministry in Rural America." Rural Matters Advocacy Paper, September 20, 2017. https://www.bgcruralmatters.

com/wp-content/uploads/2017/09    /Rural-Matters-Advocacy-Paper-Final-09.06.2016.pdf

Russell, H. H. "Small-Membership Rural Church Revitalization through Celtic Evangelism." Diss. Concordia University, 2014. ProQuest Dissertations & Theses Global (3647096). http://search.proquest.com/docview/1625748386/

Schmuck, Richard A., et al. *The Handbook of Organizational Development in Schools and Colleges: Building Regenerative Capacity.* 5th ed. Santa Cruz, CA: The Exchange Point International, 2011.

Scuderi, Noelle. "Servant Leadership and Transformational Leadership in Church Organizations." PhD diss. George Washington University, 2011. ProQuest (3413541). https://pqdtopen.proquest.com/doc/749934545.html?FMT=ABS

Sprayberry, Rodney Merrill. "The Revitalization Process in a Small Rural Plateaued Southern Baptist Church." DMin diss. Liberty University, 2010. ProQuest Dissertations & Theses Global (3398886). http://cupdx.idm.oclc.org/login?url=https://search-proquest-com.cupdx.idm .oclc.org/docview/275863123?accountid=10248

Stetzer, Ed, and Mike Dodson. *Comeback churches: How 300 Churches Turned Around and Yours Can Too.* Nashville, TN: B&H, 2007.

Stetzer, Ed, and Thom S. Rainer. *Transformational Church: Creating a New Scorecard for Congregations.* Nashville, TN: B&H, 2010.

Stroh, Elton. "Turnaround Churches in the Wisconsin Evangelical Lutheran Synod." DMin diss. Trinity International University, 2014. ProQuest Dissertations (3668860). http://search .proquest.com/docview/1648430972/

Substance Abuse and Mental Health Administration. *Results from the 2016 National Survey on Drug Use and Health: Detailed*

*Tables.* (Deliverable No. 29). Rockville, MD: Center for Behavioral Health Statistics and Quality, 2017.

United States Census Bureau. "New Census Data Show Differences between Urban and Rural Populations." (Release No. CB16–210). *American Community Survey*: 2011–2015 (December 8, 2016). https://www.census.gov/newsroom/press-releases/2016/cb16-210.html

United States Census Bureau. "Story Map Series." (n.d.). https://storymaps.geo.census.gov /arcgis /apps/MapSeries/index.html?appid=9e459da9327b4c7e9a1248cb65ad942a&cid=16O104

United States Department of Agriculture, Economic Research Center. "What Is Rural?" (2017). https://www.ers.usda.gov/topics/rural-economy-population/rural-classifications/what-is-rural.aspx

Van Dyne, Melissa, et al. *Health in Rural Missouri: Biennial Report 2016–2017.* Jefferson City, MO: Department of Health and Senior Services, Office of Primary Care and Rural Health, 2017. https://health.mo.gov/living/families/ruralhealth/pdf/biennial2017.pdf

Vaters, Karl. "Why We Stopped Taking Attendance at Our Church for a While. *Christianity Today* (August 20, 2018). https://www.christianitytoday.com/karl-vaters/2018/august /stopped-taking-attendance-church.html

Whitner, Leslie, and David McGranahan. "Rural America: Opportunities and Challenges." *Amber Waves of Grain* (February 3, 2017). https://www.ers.usda.gov/amber-waves/2003/february/rural-america/

Wood, Gene. *Leading Turnaround Churches.* Edited by Kimberly Miller; illustrated by Julie Becker. St. Charles, IL: ChurchSmart Resources, 2001.

# About the Author

D anny Davis is a rural pastor, Bible college professor, and church planting and revitalization coach. He has planted and revitalized churches in South Africa and the USA. Danny is a sought-after speaker and teacher and has travelled to multiple nations of the world to equip church leaders. Danny earned a Doctor of Education in Transformational Leadership from Concordia University–Portland. He is married to Sherry and has two adult sons.

Printed in the United States
By Bookmasters